THE MEN OF THE PACIFIC STREET SOCIAL CLUB
COOK ITALIAN

THE MEN OF
THE PACIFIC STREET
SOCIAL CLUB
COOK ITALIAN

Home-Style Recipes and Unforgettable Stories

GERARD RENNY

WILLIAM MORROW AND COMPANY, INC.   NEW YORK

It is the policy of William Morrow and Company, Inc., and its imprints and affiliates,
recognizing the importance of preserving what has been written, to print the books we publish
on acid-free paper, and we exert our best efforts to that end.

Library of Congress Cataloging-in-Publication Data has been applied for.

ISBN 0-688-15617-7

Printed in the United States of America

First Edition

1 2 3 4 5 6 7 8 9 10

BOOK DESIGN BY OKSANA KUSHNIR

www.williammorrow.com

PAST

For my mother, Jennie, and my brother Joseph—you
and others are gone but not forgotten

PRESENT

For my wife, Carolyn—my true partner in crime

FUTURE

For Max, Carmine, and Little Gerard—you don't know where
you're going unless you know where you came from

CONTENTS

Acknowledgments   xi
Introduction   1

1
MONDAY

Broiled Steak   21
Steak Pizzaiola   22
Pasta e Piselli (Pasta and Peas—2 versions)   24
Joe Red's Chicken Meatball Soup   26
Broccoli Rabe with Garlic and Red Pepper   28

2
TUESDAY

Anthony Corozzo   30
Pasta e Ceci (Pasta and Chickpea Soup)   34
Veal or Chicken Cutlets and Romaine Salad   35
   Veal or Chicken Cutlet Sandwich   36
Chicken or Veal Francese   37
Potato Croquettes   38

3
WEDNESDAY

Basic Marinara Sauce	43
Carbonara Sauce	44
Prosciutto Sauce	45
White Clam Sauce	47
Bolognese Sauce (Meat Sauce)	48
Cauliflower and Pasta Shells	50
Raw Sauce	51
Pastina for Children	52

4
THURSDAY

Joe Renny	54
Red Beef Soup	65
Macaroni Pie	66
Coyote Chicken (Roast Chicken Hunter's Style)	67
Joe Renny's Beef Stew	68

5
FRIDAY

Lentil Soup	74
Spaghettini Aglio e Olio (Thin Spaghetti with Garlic and Olive Oil)	75
Pasta Puttanesca (Spaghetti, Whore's Style— 2 versions)	76
Potatoes and Eggs	78
Eggplant Parmigiana	80
Escarole and Beans	81

6

SATURDAY

Pasta e Fagioli (Pasta and Beans) 87
Fried Pepper "Wet" Sandwich 88
Ham and Swiss Sandwich with Marinated Tomatoes 89
Stringbean Salad 90
Pickled Eggplant 91

7

SUNDAY

Sunday Gravy 98
Meatballs 99
Braciole (Stuffed Meat Rolls) 100
Lasagne 102
Pitti Boop Sandwich 104
Italian-Style Stuffed Artichokes 105

8

EASTER SUNDAY

'A Pizza Chien' (Pizza Rustica) 110
Roast Lamb with New Potatoes and Peas 112
Handmade Italian Ricotta Cavatelli (Roly Polies) 113
Manicotti (Baked Cheese-Filled Crepes
    in Tomato Sauce) 115
Desserts
Grain Pie (Lent Pie) 118
Italian Cheesecake 119
Zeppoles with Ricotta (Deep-Fried Ricotta Balls) 120

9
CHRISTMAS EVE

Crab Sauce 126

Lobster Sauce 127

Uncle Baccalà 128

Baccalà (Salt Cod, Tomato, Onion, and
Potato Casserole) 132

Fried Baccalà 133

Baccalà Salad 134

Strufolli (Honey-Coated Deep-Fried
Dough Balls) 135

Gennets (Teardrop Cookies) 137

Cenci (Deep-Fried Bows) 138

Raisin Spice Cake 140

Index 143

A C K N O W L E D G M E N T S

I have so many people to thank, I can't even tell you. It starts with all the wonderful and not-so-wonderful people in the neighborhood who made it a vital place. I mostly want to thank the wonderful ones who are still alive, such as Father Barretta. There's also, of course, my family—my mother's grandparents and her mother and her aunts who ran Pep's Restaurant, which was my inspiration for going into the restaurant business.

Of them, only Aunt Vee, age ninety-four, and Aunt Josie are still alive; Vee has given me many recipes for this book, as have my aunt Jenny and her daughter Linda. Aunt Gracie's recipes came to me through her daughter, Connie, and her sons, Buddy and Joe; and I also got recipes from Buddy's wife, Nancy. In addition to recipes, my cousin Joe Red also has a fund of good stories.

I want to thank the men of the Pacific Street Social Club for helping me find recipes and photographs that bring back the neighborhood, especially Anthony Corozzo, whom I tortured to make sure a lot of the details in the book were accurate. Joe Molinari and my cousin Richie Ciullo spent a lot of their time uncovering old photographs. Also very helpful with the recipes were Andy, Aunt Virginia, and my sister-in-law, Ticia. I don't make a move without my *consigliere,* Frank Graziadei.

I also want to thank Nancy Lindemeyer (née Canevari), who is the editor in chief of *Victoria* magazine and was instrumental in finding a publisher for this book. Nancy found me a talented recipe tester in Georgia Downard. I thank Ann Bramson, my original editor at William Morrow, who enthusiastically supported our concept, and Justin Schwartz, the editor who saw my manuscript through to the book we have today. Daniel D'Arezzo, my literary agent (also known as Odd Job), worked in several capacities to make this book happen. I thank all of my relatives on the West Coast, especially my cousin Phyllis Salaber, for coming through with photos of my uncle Ralph.

A special place of honor goes to my father, Joe Renny, who gave food a central place in my childhood, who worked hard for his family, and who instilled pride in his sons that they were Italian. Finally, I couldn't possibly have written this book, run two restaurants, and maintained any semblance of a normal life without the daily support of my very dear wife, Carolyn.

Someone from outside the neighborhood might find it very hard, if not impossible, to understand how East New York could have been a magical place. Many of the buildings still standing, brick tenements and row houses, are over a hundred years old and have fallen into disrepair; or they have been altered so as to be nearly unrecognizable from their former selves; or they have simply been torn down. An entire row of houses where my aunts and uncles and cousins once lived is now an empty lot. Worst of all, Pep's, my great-grandparents' restaurant, is now a junkyard.

In a recurring dream, I see myself reopening that restaurant. Instead of the junkyard, the two-story building—two lots wide—is there, and the grapevines still climb the fence, and women's voices murmur in the background. The women are my grandmother and her sisters and my mother, the descendants of Giuseppe (Pep) and Felicia Esposito. In addition to their four daughters—my grandmother, Mary; and my aunts Vincenza (Vee), Graziella (Gracie), and Giuseppina (Josie)—Pep and Felicia had two sons: Rafaello (Ralph), who moved west before the war and founded Florence Macaroni, and Amedeo (Meade), who became the chairman of the Democratic party in Brooklyn, or, as he liked to put it, "The Boss."

That restaurant was almost like a social club, the way it was used. There were times, particularly in the early years, during the Depression, when customers had no money and my family said, "Never mind. Pay when you can." The place was called Pep's Greasy Vest because (sad to say, but I'm telling the truth here) the patrons didn't use napkins. The women ran the restaurant, and you will find many of their recipes in this book; but you will also find recipes from my uncle Meade, as well, and from my father and from other men in the Pacific Street Social Club. Originally, many of these recipes were for banquet quantities—in servings of twenty or more—but they have been cut down to a more typical family size.

When I was born, in 1959, East New York was still an Italian enclave, and Pep's was one of many small establishments that lined the streets. Like Pep's, these others were family businesses that employed several generations. If they were lucky, the family owned the building and lived above the storefront, as did my great-grandparents with my aunt Josie and her husband and daughter.

Today, you would have to visit Italy—particularly, a city like Naples or some smaller cities and villages of the south—to understand what it was like in East New York. In Italy, as in other European countries, the small, family-owned stores, each with its specialty, still predominate. When I was a boy, the block of Eastern Parkway between Pacific and Atlantic Streets hosted a pizzeria, a fish store, the cow store (so called because of the life-size cow in the window), the pork store, Sam's High-Grade Fruits, and Mr. Lorenz's candy store. The cow

Dressed to kill. We can identify two certified (and certifiable) members of Murder, Inc., in this photo from the late 1930s: Harry "Happy" Maione, *far left*, and Vito "Chicken-head" Gurino, *third from the left*.

The garden in back of Pep's restaurant.

store was an Italian deli where you bought cheese and cold cuts and you could get sandwiches. Fat Mike owned a luncheonette on the block. He was an enormous guy and very lazy; you'd order something and he'd groan before getting up to make it for you. I once lost a baby tooth in a meatball hero from Fat Mike's—and swallowed it. At the corner was a pharmacy where people went for their remedies, since most of them couldn't afford a doctor. The pharmacist was known as Dr. Giolando. When the men played cards and the dealer asked what they needed, if a player had a really bad hand, he'd squeeze his cards hard and say, "I need Dr. Giolando"—meaning he needed a miracle.

Across the street was Carlucci's, a pizzeria/restaurant where I celebrated my fifth birthday, and around the corner was Piccolo's Poultry Store, where you could pick out a rabbit or a chicken to have fresh-killed for your dinner. I hated the smell of that place. Another famous restaurant in the neighborhood was Tex's Pizzeria on Atlantic Avenue, where some of the Brooklyn Dodgers used to hang out. And there was also The Sportsman on Fulton and Rockaway and La Casa on Eastern Parkway.

Supporting all these stores and restaurants was a community that knew how to eat. For the most part, the women did the cooking, and they did it in a very routine way. I have taken a straw poll among others who grew up in Italian neighborhoods, and my research shows that women of an earlier generation followed a strict regimen of shopping and cooking. Every day of the week, with the exception of special feast days, you knew what you were getting for dinner. Every family followed a regimen, though not necessarily the same regimen. This was ours:

MONDAY

Chicken soup
Broiled T-bone steak (medium) with chopped garlic and parsley
Mashed potatoes

———

TUESDAY

Veal cutlets
Salad
Mashed potatoes or potato croquettes

———

WEDNESDAY

Pasta with marinara or leftover Sunday gravy

———

THURSDAY

Chicken, coyote style, or beef stew

———

FRIDAY

Takeout pizza or
potatoes and eggs

———

SATURDAY

Cold cuts
Wet sandwich
Hearty soup in winter

———

SUNDAY

Sunday gravy

The reason for the pizza or potatoes and eggs on Friday was that the Roman Catholic Church's dietary restriction on meats was still in effect and I didn't like fish, so I went both meatless and fishless on Fridays. The reason for the cold cuts on Saturday nights was that my mother spent all day Saturday preparing the Sunday gravy, and we kids spent all day playing, eating, and running in and out of the restaurant. Sunday was, in its way, our weekly feast day.

The unvarying menu in our home never induced boredom; we always seemed to have enough variety. Like the food my friends and I ate at home while growing up, the recipes in this book are simple, hearty, and delicious. The basic principle of Italian cooking is to start with good ingredients and not ruin them. We found those good ingredients in abundance in the neighborhood stores, but they were not fancy ingredients: My mother cooked with pure or blended olive oil, never with extra-virgin olive oil. As I got older, and my palate grew more sophisticated,

It was a rare occasion when my great-grandparents entertained in the apartment above Pep's restaurant, and this was one of them: My uncle Ralph (seated at the head of the table, his mother and father on his right) and his family visiting Brooklyn from California around 1947.

The neighborhood pastime. Men shooting craps at the corner of Powell Street and East New York Avenue. They're well dressed because it's Sunday and they've been to church. Standing on the sidewalk are Al and Jimmy Ciullo.

One day, in the late 1940s, Al and Jimmy were shooting craps with Harry "Pittsburgh Phil" Strauss, who was losing and getting madder and madder. So Al whispered to Jimmy, "On the count of three, take the money and run." They got away with it that time.

I used extra-virgin, which is heavier and has a richer flavor. What's most important is the skill in cooking that was handed down from generation to generation and is available to anyone who truly likes to eat.

We were equally unpretentious in the way we talked about food. In Italy, over 600 types of pasta are made; we called all pasta *macaroni*. We never referred to pasta sauce; it was simply "gravy." And I never tasted *pesto* until I was an adult. Pesto, which I love, is a Genovese dish, and much of the Italian cuisine that is known and celebrated in America today is of northern, particularly Tuscan, origin. But the fact of the matter is that most Italian Americans come from places like Naples and Sicily and Bari, and this book is a celebration of our southern heritage.

East New York is the easternmost part of Brooklyn, which is a mythical place in the imaginations of innumerable sons and daughters of immigrants, mainly Irish, Jewish, and Italian. The sector I grew up in is part of Community District 6. It's a small quadrant northeast of Crown Heights, northwest of Brownsville, southeast of Bedford-Stuyvesant, southwest of Bushwick. To the east, it runs into Queens, and eastward is where the Italians largely went when they left— to Ozone Park and Howard Beach and small towns in western Nassau County. There is nothing famous in East New York, nothing you would go out of your way to see. It is the middle of nowhere. The Long Island Rail Road passes by along Atlantic Avenue carrying passengers from Pennsylvania Station, in Manhattan, all the way out to Montauk on the far east end of Long Island; but the train

Cars are always a big deal in a poor neighborhood. Since most people didn't own their own homes, a car was the biggest thing they could afford. You'd look at a guy like the one pictured here (I'm not sure what make and model he's driving) and you'd say, "What a car! What a guy!"

is underground here, and the passengers do not look up from their newspapers to view the twin towers of Our Lady of Loreto on the corner of Sackman Avenue and Pacific Street.

Before it was Italian, the neighborhood was predominantly Irish. What it was before then I don't know—maybe there was nothing here but farmland. For most of the nineteenth century, Irish immigrants far outnumbered Italians. But in the decade of the 1890s, that trend reversed itself. And between 1890 and 1950, five times as many Italians as Irish immigrated here. The vast majority of Italians came between 1890 and 1920, which marked the heyday of Italian-American Brooklyn. In addition to East New York, Italians also settled in Red Hook, Benson-hurst, and Brownsville.

And Brooklyn was not the only place Italians settled. There were large communities on Manhattan's Lower East Side, in Little Italy, in Greenwich Village, and in East Harlem. In Queens there was Astoria; in the Bronx, Morris Park. Although New York City hosted the largest population of Italians in America (in 1915 New York had more Italians than Palermo), many other cities had Italian neighborhoods: in the East, Boston, Hartford, Bridgeport, Providence, Philadelphia, Pittsburgh (where my father came from), Baltimore; in the Midwest, Chicago, Cleveland, Cincinnati, Youngstown, Steubenville; and out west, San Francisco and the Wine Country in California.

In some of these places, you find stronger traces of the Italian past, but fre-

The Feast of San Pasquale in the 1940s.

Say "cheese." Jenny Janace, the Cow Store Lady, and family.

quently (as in North Beach or Little Italy) the past is embalmed for the tourists. In places like East New York, the past has entirely vanished. The latest census figures show that, while the overall population of Community District 6 grew 15 percent between 1980 and 1990, the non-Hispanic white population (Italians, Irish, Germans) declined 39 percent. The population is now about 80 percent non-Hispanic black and 18 percent Hispanic. Italian Americans have dwindled to a few widows like Fanny DiNapoli and Graziella Tirino, who cling to the same houses in which they have lived for forty or fifty years.

The Jews are ghettoized in Crown Heights. The Irish left long ago. The years that I was growing up, in the 1960s and early 1970s, were a period of radical change. The Italian neighborhoods were the victims of successful integration. Unfortunately, assimilation came at a cost. We lost a lot of our traditions; we lost our language; we lost our vital communities.

Like so many others who achieved prosperity, Italian Americans moved to the suburbs. My parents left the old neighborhood when I was twelve years old. Pep's closed its doors the following year. My mother died a year later, and the world I had known ended.

The complex relationship between the Irish and Italians is not unique. The Irish, who had been underdogs in America, had risen to places of prominence in New York—notably in politics, the police force, and the pulpit—by the time the Italians started coming over in great numbers. The Italians were the new underdogs, and although they shared the same religion with the Irish, they were treated as badly by the Irish as the Irish themselves had been treated. (There's a picture on the opposite page of Molinari's Saloon and the two brothers who ran it: a couple of "Mustache Petes," as they were called, one of whom was forced to return to Italy because he had killed in the saloon an Irish cop who had called him a "guinea.") But because of the massive numbers arriving from Italy, the Italians were able to build their own churches, and start their own gangs. Because they couldn't trust the Irish cops, they relied on their local "made guys" (a man who had made himself by rising through the mob's ranks) to resolve disputes.

Those gangs started out as American branches of Sicilian Mafia or Neapolitan Camorra, and they had old-country ways. They were clannish, suspicious, and limited to the neighborhoods they controlled. During Prohibition, they were all involved in the bootleg gin business, which inevitably led to gang warfare between rival mobs. But with the end of Prohibition in 1933 (and the end of easy money), a more sophisticated criminal league took over from the Mustache Petes—the Combination.

Sixty years ago East New York was the home base of Brooklyn's "Murder, Inc.," the enforcement arm of a resurgent nationwide syndicate that called itself "the Combination." This was an organization of crime lords in the major American cities who had banded together to impose order on the pursuit of power and ill-gotten wealth. The tabloids named our local branch Murder, Inc., because it ruthlessly exercised control through terror—and the East New York branch consisted primarily of enforcers. The mean streets of East New York had bred killers

Two "Mustache Petes," the Molinari brothers, founded the saloon that later became the funeral home. It is still there, one of the last vestiges of the old neighborhood.

like Harry Maione (called "Happy" Maione because he was such a miserable son of a bitch) and Frank (the Dasher) Abbandando, both of whom Brooklyn's U.S. District Attorney (and later mayor of New York) William O'Dwyer sent to the electric chair for rubbing out their cohort George Rudnick in 1937. Maione, Abbandando, Vito (Chickenhead) Gurino, Harry (Pittsburgh Phil) Strauss, and others had, of course, been responsible for countless other murders. Their captain was a distant cousin of mine, Louis Capone (no relation to Al). But family ties were of little consequence when they conflicted with the demands of the Combination. My great-granduncle, Pep's brother, was a small-time operator who somehow got into a dispute with some wiseguys. One day he was walking his dog across Pacific Street. They shot him dead in the street. For good measure, they also shot the dog. Years afterward, when I was a kid, my friends and I found a human skull in a backyard. We found some other bones, too. Who knows what you'd find if you started digging up backyards and cellars in that neighborhood?

Ironically, it was through successful prosecutions for the murders of their fellow mobsters that O'Dwyer broke the back of Murder, Inc. Even killing other criminals is still a crime. And the terror these wiseguys spread was so pervasive that the community finally turned on them by giving a pass to those who, threatened with death by the Combination, turned state's evidence. After Lou Capone was electrocuted, his wife, Mary, walked around with a gun and threatened to kill the guys who had ratted on her husband—but she never did.

For the past thirty years, social clubs have gotten a bad rap—though not without some cause. When I was growing up, the social clubs in East New York were, in fact, linked to the underworld syndicate. But most social club members weren't criminals; they were "knockaround" guys—stand-up guys, good guys who knew what it took to make a living and did what they had to do. They were bus drivers and construction workers and shopkeepers. They had colorful (often very accurate) nicknames—Beanzy, Kid Gap, Junior Baccalà, Popeye, Squinty, Beep, Quack Quack, Willie Hop, Chi Chi, Tony Shovels (Tony, for example, had huge hands). They were men who wanted a place to go, other than the corner, to hang out. The clubs were a replacement for the Neapolitan bars (not really like American bars—more like a café that serves wine, beer, aperitifs, and even ice cream as well as coffee and pastries) where everyone went after dinner to talk and play cards. Social clubs were a poor man's country club. In the early days, they were based on particular towns—there were clubs for the Neapolitans, for the Pomiglianese, for the Potenzanos. There were some Sicilians as well. After a couple of generations, the families had intermarried and other connections took precedence—whom you grew up with, whom you were related to. Social clubs sprang from the need men have to escape from homes ruled by women and to enjoy male companionship—the need for a place where they can play cards and not be asked to take out the garbage. As Chaucer wrote six centuries ago in "The Wife of Bath's Tale," what a woman wants is "sovereignty" in her own home. Italian families tended to be highly compartmentalized: Men's and women's domains were strictly delineated, and women unquestionably held sway in the kitchen.

Social clubs, not least of all, gave men an opportunity to exercise their culinary skills. In the clubs, men cooked for each other, sharing familiar dishes with the variations they had learned from their mothers. Sometimes a simple variation could change your life. I recall as a boy eating at a friend's house, and his mother surprised me by putting a bowl of ricotta cheese on the table along with the rigatoni and meat sauce. I loved it. And I went rushing home to tell my mother about my wonderful discovery. At the social clubs, men made their favorite foods and made them in the quantities men liked, on the general theory that too much is not enough.

The new Pacific Street Social Club came into being when Stanley Molinari died in 1993. During Prohibition, the Molinaris had changed from saloonkeepers to undertakers. Stanley was the second in the line, and he had buried a great number of my friends and relatives, including my mother and my older brother Joseph. Many of us were gathered at the Molinari Funeral Home to mark Stanley's passing, officiated by Father Barretta, who had ministered, for as long as I could remember, to the flock of Our Lady of Loreto, across the street from Molinari's. (It was Stanley's father who had donated the land for the church, which was built on that site in 1925, though it was founded in 1894.)

Several of my friends from the neighborhood, many of them somewhat older than I, with longer memories—Stanley's son Joe, Anthony and Blaise Corozzo, my cousin Joe Red, Buster, Lenny Isch, Nealy Bonehead—met again in the neighborhood most of us had left behind. With Stanley's death, we keenly felt the passing of a generation, the passing of the traditions that had educated us. The

The Pacific Street Social Club today, in the Knights of Columbus Hall in East New York.

Jeep Jr. and Nealy Bonehead.

Christmas at the Pacific Street Social Club.

The Club today. *Left to right:* Nealy Bonehead, Blaise Corozzo, Salvator Reggio, Anthony Corozzo.

buildings are still there on the desolate streets, including the "*Palazzo di Napoli*," an ironic nickname for the big tenement in which my family had its ground-floor apartment. That block on Dean Street was my world. We played slap ball and punch ball, keeping an eye out for cars, and at one end of the building across the street, we lined up to play Johnny-on-the-Pony, in which one team tried to form a human wall and the other team tried to break it down. In summertime watermelons were kept in a vacant lot across the way, and we would steal a melon and break it open against that same building's end, eating the warm melon and spitting out the seeds while the sweet water dribbled down our chins. Also, in summertime, we opened up the fire hydrant—we called it a "Johnny pump"—and played in the spray. When I was very small, I decided to test myself against the force of the spray; naturally, it blew me across the street. If my older brother Joseph had not been there and jumped out to stop a car that was coming down our street, I may not have been here today.

Those were among the happiest times in my life. It was (all appearances to the contrary) a secure world. I knew everyone and was related to half of them. We attended church together, went to the same parochial schools, and celebrated the same feast days. My grandmother's restaurant was across the street, and I ran in there when I was hungry or thirsty or wanted company. The other guys in the neighborhood did the same thing; they too grew up with my grandmother's cooking. I savor the smells of that world, I relish the taste. It's hardly to be wondered that I gravitated to the restaurant business and have my own restaurants.

When my friends and I saw that our traditions would vanish without a ripple, we decided, then and there at Stanley's funeral, to reestablish our old social club. The club, next to where Rose Sasso's bakery had been and half a block from Our Lady of Loreto, is on Pacific Street between Sackman and Stone Avenues. It's just a converted storefront with a tile floor and tin ceiling. The furniture is mix and match; there's a jukebox, a cigarette machine, espresso maker. We have whiskey and beer on hand, and plenty of coffee. On Thursday nights, this is where we have gathered, to reminisce and to catch up on our current situations and to eat and drink and play cards in the time-honored tradition.

We have also revived the tradition of celebrating feast days with food served in the street. The feast days were the ones the original immigrants brought from their hometowns. Many had come from Potenza, in the southern Apennines, and celebrated the Feast of Our Lady of the Angels. Those who hailed from Pomigliano, in the hills of the Campania, celebrated San Pasquale. The Neapolitans, of course, celebrated San Gennaro, patron saint of their fair city. My family, because we had so many Josephs (my great-grandfather Pep; my father, Joe Renny; and my brother Joseph), celebrated St. Joseph's Day on March 19. The vast majority of people in my neighborhood were, like my mother's family, Pomiglianese; my father's family came from Benevento, farther east and higher in the mountains. The principal feast days, however, were Christmas Eve and Easter Sunday, and to these I have devoted a chapter each.

Food is not only the staff of life, it is also the stuff of story. While giving you recipes for the food we ate, I also share with you some of my memories. This is a practical cookbook, and anyone can be successful with these simple recipes. It is a cookbook you will use, because the food is simple, good, nourishing, and delicious. It is also a cookbook you can sit back and read to experience a vanished world. It is my hope that, like the village in *Brigadoon*, that world will come to life for you once in a while in a steaming broth or a mouthful of Sunday gravy.

MONDAY

Monday night was meat night. We had a soup and then some kind of beef—either a broiled T-bone or steak pizzaiola. The latter was my father's creation. After my mother died, when I was fourteen, Joe Renny cooked dinner for me as his way of restoring order and keeping the family together. My father wasn't a psychologist, but he knew instinctively that the best thing for us was to sit down together for a meal. In its way, his steak pizzaiola worked. We have been through a lot as a family, and it hasn't always been easy, but we're still together.

Marriage Italian-American style. My cousin Joe Red, and his wife, Josephine, in 1962. Childhood sweethearts, they're still married, with two daughters and three grandchildren.

Tony "the Barber" in drag, with Aunt Gracie on Halloween.

BROILED STEAK

Successful steaks start with good cuts of meat that aren't cut too thin. They should be at least ¾ inch thick, or they will cook through before they are nicely browned on the outside. There are several variables peculiar to each oven: whether gas or electric, how far the heat is from the steak, how hot it gets inside the broiler. You just have to experiment until you come up with the right cooking time.

MAKES 4 SERVINGS

2 tablespoons extra-virgin olive oil
Four 10- to 12-ounce steaks, T-bone
   or sirloin

4 cloves garlic, chopped
¼ cup chopped fresh parsley
Salt and freshly ground black pepper

1. Preheat the broiler.

2. Rub ¼ tablespoon of the olive oil on both sides of each steak. Then rub them with chopped garlic, ½ clove to each side, and sprinkle with parsley. Add salt and pepper to taste and place the steaks on a cookie sheet, broiling pan, or baking dish. Put the steaks in the broiler and, turning them once, cook for 4 to 5 minutes on each side.

STEAK PIZZAIOLA

So far as I know, Worcestershire sauce is not an Italian condiment. But it was typical of the Italian Americans to incorporate new things into their cooking. And for that matter, we hardly ate Italian-style cooking all the time. This was Brooklyn, after all, and we enjoyed the varied cuisine of a diverse city, including the best knishes in the entire world. At least one day a week, we'd "eat American," and we often ate hot dogs for lunch. We also went out for Chinese food all the time. So why wouldn't my father use Worcestershire sauce? The key is to coat the steak thoroughly with the sauce and to get it nicely browned.

MAKES 6 SERVINGS

¼ cup olive oil
10 cloves garlic, crushed
One 2- to 2¼-pound flank steak or
    London broil, cut into 10
    (scaloppine-size) slices
Salt and freshly ground black pepper
¼ cup Worcestershire sauce

Two 28-ounce cans crushed tomatoes
    (not in puree)
1½ teaspoons dried oregano
Cooked pasta, extra-virgin olive oil,
    and freshly grated Parmesan cheese
    as accompaniments, if desired

1. In a large, deep skillet or casserole set over moderately high heat, heat half the oil until it is hot. Add the garlic and cook, stirring, until golden, 30 to 60 seconds.

2. Sprinkle the steak with salt and pepper to taste. Add half the steak to the skillet, season the top with half the Worcestershire sauce, or to taste, and fry the steak until browned on both sides, 2 to 3 minutes per side. Transfer to a platter. Add

the remaining oil to the pan and heat it until hot. Add the remaining steak and Worcestershire and fry as above. Transfer to a platter.

3. Add the tomatoes, oregano, and salt and pepper to the skillet and bring to a boil, scraping up brown bits clinging to bottom of pan. Reduce the heat and simmer for 20 minutes.

4. Return the steak along with accumulated juices from the platter to the skillet, spooning the sauce over the steak. Simmer uncovered, turning occasionally, until the meat is tender, 1 to 1¼ hours.

5. To serve, add some of the sauce to cooked pasta, drizzle with a little extra-virgin olive oil, and toss. Or, serve with mashed potatoes or potato croquettes. Spinach or broccoli rabe makes a nice accompaniment. Pass Parmesan cheese separately at the table.

PASTA E PISELLI
Pasta and Peas

Here are two versions of a dish made in every Italian household in our neighborhood: one version with chicken broth, the other with tomato sauce. Everyone experimented with Pasta and Peas, throwing in whatever they had that added something. I prefer LeSueur canned peas, but use whatever you like. In the tomato version, the peas, which lend color as well as protein, are added to the sauce at the end so they remain whole.

CHICKEN BROTH VERSION
MAKES 6 SERVINGS

3 tablespoons olive oil
3 cloves garlic, sliced
1 onion, chopped
1 cup chicken broth
One 15-ounce can LeSueur or similar
    peas, including the liquid
1 teaspoon dried oregano
Salt and freshly ground black pepper

1 cup small tubular pasta, such as
    tubetti or ditalini
½ cup freshly grated Romano or
    Parmesan cheese, plus additional
    cheese for serving
Minced fresh parsley and basil leaves
    for garnish

1. In a saucepan set over moderate heat, heat the oil until hot. Add the garlic and cook, stirring, until pale golden, about 2 minutes. Add the onion and cook, stirring, until softened, about 3 minutes. Add the broth, peas with liquid, oregano, and salt and pepper to taste, and bring to a boil. Reduce the heat to low and simmer, stirring occasionally, for 20 minutes.

2. Meanwhile, cook the pasta according to package directions and drain. Return the pasta to the pan, add the sauce along with the cheese, and toss to combine. Transfer the pasta to a serving dish and sprinkle with the parsley and basil, to taste. Pass additional cheese at the table.

TOMATO SAUCE VERSION
MAKES 4 SERVINGS

¼ cup olive oil
1 large clove garlic, sliced
1 onion, thinly sliced
2 cups Basic Marinara Sauce (page 43) or store-bought fresh marinara sauce
1 cup small tubular pasta, such as tubetti or ditalini

One 15-ounce can LeSueur or similar peas, including the liquid
¼ cup freshly grated Parmesan or Romano cheese, plus additional cheese for serving

1. In a saucepan set over moderate heat, heat the oil until hot. Add the garlic and cook, stirring, until golden, about 2 minutes. Add the onion and cook, stirring occasionally, until golden brown, 5 to 7 minutes. Add the tomato sauce and bring to a boil. Reduce the heat to low and simmer, stirring occasionally, for 20 minutes. Add the peas and simmer for 10 minutes more.

2. Meanwhile, cook the pasta according to package directions and drain. Add the pasta to the sauce along with the cheese and stir to combine. Transfer to a serving dish and pass additional cheese at the table.

JOE RED'S CHICKEN MEATBALL SOUP

Joe Red is my cousin, Aunt Gracie's son, and this recipe, for which he is famous at the social club, came from his mother. Gracie was famous as well for her vegetable soup, which she made in huge quantities and sent around the neighborhood to friends and family in Mason jars. She had quite a mouth on her. She liked to joke with us kids that she could bottle her soup and sell it as "Gracie's alla f*#!ing vegetable soup." And she laughed when we looked shocked that an old lady could swear.

MAKES 6 SERVINGS

FOR THE STOCK

One 3- to 3½-pound chicken, rinsed
1 onion, studded with 4 cloves
1 celery stalk, cut into thick slices
½ carrot, cut into thick slices
1 bay leaf
1 teaspoon dried thyme
8 black peppercorns
8 to 10 cups cold water
Salt

FOR THE MEATBALLS

1¼ pounds ground chicken (or lean
    ground beef)
3 slices white bread, cubed and
    soaked in ¼ cup milk

¼ cup dry bread crumbs
2 large eggs, lightly beaten
½ cup freshly grated Romano cheese
½ cup minced fresh parsley leaves
1 tablespoon minced garlic
½ teaspoon salt, or to taste
¼ teaspoon freshly ground black pepper

FOR THE SOUP

1 onion, cut into large dice
6 carrots, sliced thick
1 celery heart (6 stalks), sliced thick
1 tablespoon minced garlic
½ cup minced fresh parsley leaves
Freshly grated Parmesan cheese as an
    accompaniment

1. First, make the stock. In a casserole or stockpot, combine all of the stock ingredients with enough cold water to cover, and bring to a boil. Skim the surface of foam, reduce the heat, and simmer, continuing to skim frequently, 1½ to 2 hours, or until the chicken is very tender. Remove the chicken and transfer to a plate. Strain the stock through a large sieve, return to the casserole, and cook at a boil until reduced to 10 cups, 5 to 10 minutes. Correct the seasoning, adding more salt and pepper to taste. Remove the skin and bones from the chicken, shred into bite-size pieces and reserve.

2. While the stock is simmering, make the meatballs. In a bowl, combine all of the meatball ingredients and with wet hands form into balls about 1 inch in diameter. Chill until ready to cook.

3. Next, make the soup. To the simmering stock add the vegetables and garlic, and bring to a boil. Reduce the heat and simmer for 20 minutes. Add the meatballs and simmer for an additional 20 minutes. Add the reserved chicken and simmer until heated through. Before serving, stir in the parsley. Serve the soup with the Parmesan.

BROCCOLI RABE WITH GARLIC
AND RED PEPPER

Traditionally a side dish, broccoli rabe can be a meal in itself served with bread. The olive oil combined with the water in the vegetable makes a delicious broth. My father would pour on enough red pepper flakes to burn down a building, and that could be his dinner on a Saturday afternoon.

MAKES 4 TO 6 SERVINGS

2 small bunches or 1 large bunch broccoli rabe, trimmed and rinsed
¼ cup extra-virgin olive oil

3 cloves garlic, sliced thin
Red pepper flakes
Salt

1. In a large saucepan fitted with a steaming rack, heat 2 inches of water over very high heat. Arrange the broccoli rabe on the rack and steam, covered, for 6 to 7 minutes, or until the greens are just tender. Alternatively, place the broccoli rabe in a large saucepan filled with boiling salted water. Blanch, uncovered, for 4 to 5 minutes, or until just tender. Drain the broccoli rabe and set aside.

2. Meanwhile, in a small skillet set over moderate heat, heat the oil and cook the garlic, stirring, until it's golden, about 2 minutes. Add the red pepper flakes to taste.

3. Transfer the broccoli rabe to a serving plate, season with salt to taste, and spoon the hot flavored oil over the vegetables.

2

TUESDAY

I have no idea why this was chicken or veal night in our household. Basically, there were just a couple of ways the cutlets were cooked, none of them very fancy. In essence, these are quick and easy recipes. The cutlets were usually served with a salad and with potato croquettes, often made with leftover mashed potatoes from the night before.

ANTHONY COROZZO

Anthony is the glue that holds the neighborhood together. No matter how far from the neighborhood everyone goes, Anthony always stays in touch. And if the neighborhood were a museum, Anthony would be the curator. Here he is in his own words:

As a kid I worked at the New York Public Library—the main library on Forty-second Street—and I clerked on Wall Street for a while. But I didn't like working for other people and always wanted to have my own business. I tried a lot of them: a hair salon, a jewelry store, a restaurant. I had vending machines for a while. I always wanted to be an actor, but I was too shy to do anything about it. Then a friend of mine dragged me down to a casting call, and I started getting parts as an extra. That's what I do now, and I love it.

I've been in about sixty movies now, mostly as an extra, but I've had speaking roles in a few, starting with *A Bronx Tale* in 1992. I went to the casting call late, toward the end, but Robert De Niro picked me out right away. And once he started shooting the movie, my character became more developed. He had

Anthony today, curator of East New York.

me doing more than the script originally called for, but a lot of those scenes got cut. I'm a principal character, but you have to watch pretty close to see me. Since then I've had speaking roles in *The Deli, Donnie Brasco, Men Lie,* and a TV miniseries, *Witness to the Mob,* among others. Mainly, I'm typecast as a stand-up kind of guy in movies about Italian Americans.

When I was born, the youngest of four boys, we were living on Pitkin Avenue in the Brownsville section of Brooklyn. Later on we moved up Eastern Parkway to

Anthony's father, Lefty Corozzo, *left*, with Joe Brown. Joe was Italian—maybe his family name had been Bruno. In Brooklyn, he was a Brown.

Ocean Hill, and I attended school at Our Lady of Loreto and then Franklin K. Lane High School, which at the time was academically one of the highest rated schools in New York City. My father was a laborer in the construction business, and we never had much money. My mother cooked for us the same thing, pretty much, for every night of the week. In our house, though, Thursday was macaroni night, and Saturday we'd eat American, maybe a steak, if things were good. Sunday, of course, was the whole big traditional meal.

As kids, we lived for the A train, which stops at Broadway Junction. It took us everywhere. In summer we were on the streets day and night, and when we were teenagers we took the A train to Rockaway Beach every day. A group from the neighborhood went together, and we had our neighborhood section at the beach, with a jukebox on the boardwalk and dancing and making out with the girls. And then the A train took us into the city at night. We'd go to a movie on Forty-second Street, then down to Chinatown for dinner. Chinese food was our favorite, and we used to say we were going out for Chinks. It was shorthand, not prejudice.

My favorite holiday was Christmas because school was out and we partied day and night. Christmas Eve was special because you spent the entire evening with your family. We went to midnight Mass at Our Lady of Loreto, then we walked around the neighborhood and stopped at everyone's house for a drink. Even the kids had a drink. If you were nine or older, you had a glass of wine and by the end of the evening you were drunk.

The social clubs were an everyday version of that kind of socializing. The men went out almost every night. Nobody stood home. After dinner, a man said to his wife, "I'm going to the corner." Maybe the corner was twenty blocks away, where he had his club. You couldn't smoke a cigar at home, so you smoked it at the club. And then you'd play cards. The old guys played a game called "brisk," or sometimes they played *tre sette*. We usually played poker or gin rummy. And later on, in the '70s and '80s, some of the guys started playing continental. There was always a bookie and everybody bet on the horses or sports. There was always a crap game too. Some guys could get so involved in a game they'd stay up the whole night and sleep the next day.

Tending the roses.

So that's what we did for entertainment during the week. And on weekends we might decide to go to Tony's Cabaret on Atlantic Avenue and Eastern Parkway. He booked some comics and singers. The Bari Trio, a group from the neighborhood, played there. Most of the bars had a place for bocce in the back. In the '50s, I remember, some of them had signs out that said, "Ladies Welcome." That was a big innovation back then.

Sometimes I do a little cooking at the club. My favorite meal, no question, is *past' e cic'*.

Anthony's uncle John Corozzo, *left*, with his friend Terry at
Herkimer Street and Haven's Place.

PASTA E CECI
Pasta and Chickpea Soup

This is a favorite at the social club, halfway between a pasta dish and a soup.

MAKES 6 SERVINGS

⅓ cup olive oil
6 cloves garlic, smashed
One 19-ounce can chickpeas,
    drained
Salt and freshly ground pepper

4 cups chicken broth
½ pound small pasta shells
½ cup freshly grated Parmesan, plus
    additional for serving

1. In a saucepan set over moderate heat, heat the oil until hot. Add the garlic and cook, stirring, until golden brown on all sides, about 2 minutes. Add the chickpeas and salt and pepper to taste and cook, stirring, for 3 minutes more. Add the broth and bring to a boil. Reduce the heat to low and simmer, covered, for 15 minutes.

2. With a slotted spoon, remove about one quarter of the chickpeas and puree in a blender, food processor, or food mill, or mash with a fork. Return the chickpea puree to the soup and bring to a boil over moderate heat, stirring occasionally. Add the pasta and simmer, covered, until the pasta is al dente. Off the heat, stir in the cheese and let stand for 2 to 3 minutes to develop flavor and texture.

3. Ladle the soup into bowls and serve with additional Parmesan.

VEAL OR CHICKEN CUTLETS
AND ROMAINE SALAD

This is the basic recipe for veal and chicken cutlets in our home—a poor man's version of the veal milanese served in restaurants with arugula, tomatoes, and onion. My grandmother made the Veal Cutlet Sandwich (see below) by mixing the salad ingredients with her hands, which were seasoned by years of food preparation. We thought that's what gave her sandwiches their special flavor.

MAKES 4 SERVINGS

1 cup Italian seasoned bread crumbs
2 tablespoons freshly grated Parmesan
   cheese
¼ teaspoon garlic powder
Salt and freshly ground black pepper
1 cup all-purpose flour
3 large eggs

1 pound veal cutlets (cut from the
   leg), pounded very thin, or 1
   pound chicken cutlets (from the
   breast), pounded very thin
About 1 cup olive oil for frying
Romaine Salad (recipe follows)

1. On a plate, combine the bread crumbs, Parmesan, garlic powder, and salt and pepper to taste. On another plate, sprinkle the flour into an even layer. In a shallow bowl beat the eggs. Lightly dredge each veal (or chicken) cutlet in the flour, dip in the egg, letting the excess drip off, and coat with the bread crumbs.

2. In a large skillet set over moderately high heat, heat 2 to 3 tablespoons olive oil until hot. Add the veal cutlets and cook them, in batches, adding more oil as necessary, until the cutlets are golden brown on the undersides, 2 to 3 minutes.

continued

Turn the veal cutlets and cook until crisp, 1 to 2 minutes more. Transfer to a platter and serve with the salad.

ROMAINE SALAD
MAKES 4 TO 6 SERVINGS

2 hearts of romaine (inner leaves), chopped
½ cup extra-virgin olive oil

¼ cup red wine vinegar
Salt and freshly ground pepper

In a bowl, combine all the ingredients. You may use more or less oil, vinegar, and salt and pepper, to taste.

VEAL OR CHICKEN CUTLET SANDWICH
MAKES 4 SERVINGS

One 16-inch loaf Italian bread, such as semolina

1. Prepare veal or chicken cutlets, as shown above.

2. Split the loaf of bread in half lengthwise, leaving one side attached so that the bread is hinged. Remove some of the inside crumb from each loaf to create a trench for the sandwich filling.

3. Make the romaine salad, as shown above. (The salad should be wet enough to soak into the bread for a moist sandwich.)

4. Divide the romaine among the loaves and top with a layer of veal cutlets (about 2 to 3 per sandwich). Cut each loaf crosswise into 4 portions and transfer to serving plates.

CHICKEN OR VEAL FRANCESE

This version is one that my mother never used; it came from a cousin whose mother used it to vary the menu for their family when she was bored making veal cutlets the traditional way.

MAKES 4 SERVINGS

6 large eggs
3 tablespoons freshly grated Parmesan
  cheese
Salt and freshly ground pepper
All-purpose flour for dredging
1 pound chicken or veal cutlets,
  pounded thin and cut into small
  pieces, about 5 inches square

3 tablespoons olive oil
1 to 1½ sticks unsalted butter
Juice from 2 lemons

continued

1. In a shallow bowl, whisk together the eggs, Parmesan, and salt and pepper to taste. In another shallow bowl or on a plate, sprinkle the flour.

2. Dredge the cutlets first in the flour, then in the egg mixture, letting the excess drip off, and finally back in the flour, coating each piece well.

3. In a large skillet set over moderately high heat, heat 2 tablespoons of the olive oil until hot.

4. Dip the flour-coated cutlets once again into the egg mixture and add them to the pan, in batches. Cook the cutlets until golden brown, about 1 minute on each side. Transfer the cutlets to a large plate when browned, and fry the remaining pieces in the same manner. Add more oil as necessary.

5. Add the butter to the skillet and melt it over moderate heat. Return the cutlets to the pan, turning to coat them with the butter, and cook until heated through, about 2 minutes. Transfer the meat to serving plates, add the lemon juice to the pan, and swirl the sauce until combined well. Spoon the sauce over the cutlets and serve immediately.

POTATO CROQUETTES

I don't know the origin of potato croquettes, but they're served as a side dish at some good Neapolitan restaurants here in New York, at Patsy's in midtown or Angelo's in the Village. We had them on Monday nights with steak pizzaiola or on Tuesdays with veal cutlets. No ordinary croquettes—the little piece of mozzarella in the middle is like a special bonus.

2 large Idaho or Russet potatoes (about 1 to 1¼ pounds), cooked and mashed; or 2 cups mashed potatoes
½ cup freshly grated Parmesan cheese, or to taste
1 large egg, lightly beaten
Salt and freshly ground black pepper

4 to 6 ounces mozzarella cheese, cut into sticks 2½ inches long and ¼ inch thick

FOR THE COATING

All-purpose flour for dredging
2 large eggs, lightly beaten
1 to 1¼ cups fine dry bread crumbs
Olive oil for frying

1. In a bowl, combine the potatoes, Parmesan, egg, and salt and pepper to taste. With dampened hands, form the mixture into logs about 3 inches long and ½ to ¾ inch in diameter. Press a stick of mozzarella down the center of each log and re-form the potato mixture around the cheese to enclose it.

2. For the coating, dredge the croquettes in the flour, shaking off the excess, dip them in the eggs, and coat them in the bread crumbs. Transfer the croquettes to a large plate and let chill for at least 30 minutes.

3. In a large, preferably nonstick, skillet set over moderately high heat, heat ¼ inch of olive oil until hot. Add the croquettes and fry them, in batches, turning, until golden brown on all sides, 5 to 6 minutes. Serve as a side dish to meats or poultry.

3

WEDNESDAY

Wednesday was Prince Spaghetti Day in many parts of the Northeast because a smart advertising agency tapped into the Italian-American neighborhood tradition of having pasta on Wednesday night. Some of the guys I've talked with had pasta on Tuesdays or Thursdays. Pasta was a mainstay in our family. But we didn't call it pasta; it was macaroni, and the sauce was called "gravy." There were several kinds of sauces, usually derived from a basic marinara; and we cooked dried pasta. In fact, my uncle Ralph went to the West Coast and started making dried pasta—Florence Macaroni—in the Watts area of Los Angeles, and he was one of the first to make pasta flavored with spinach, artichoke, and tomato. (For recipes for fresh pasta, see Lasagna Noodles (page 103), Handmade Italian Ricotta Cavatelli (page 113), and Manicotti (page 115).

The pasta of choice was usually linguine or spaghetti, cooked al dente, well drained, and mixed with the sauce, which was also served on the side. But we ate other kinds of macaroni, and each sauce comes with a recommended pasta.

Ray Muscarella in the doorway to Pep's garden.

BASIC MARINARA SAUCE

This is the basic tomato sauce that can be used by itself or in combination with other things—for example, see the recipe for Cauliflower and Pasta Shells (page 50) or the recipes in Chapter 7 for Meatballs (page 99) and Braciole (page 100). To make the popular penne alla vodka, for example, you simply heat a little vodka in a skillet, add some marinara, toss in the cooked penne, and finish with a touch of cream. Marinara freezes well and can be made in quantity and stored in the quantity you most often use.

MAKES 4 TO 6 SERVINGS

¼ cup extra-virgin olive oil

8 cloves garlic, smashed

1 onion, minced

Two 28-ounce cans crushed tomatoes or whole canned tomatoes, gently crushed with your hands

1½ teaspoons dried oregano, or 1 tablespoon fresh minced oregano

Salt and freshly ground pepper

Red pepper flakes (optional)

1 pound pasta

Sliced basil leaves for garnish (optional)

Freshly grated Parmesan cheese, as an accompaniment

1. In a deep skillet set over moderate heat, heat 2 tablespoons of the oil until hot. Add the garlic and onion and cook, stirring occasionally, until they're pale golden, 5 to 7 minutes. Add the tomatoes, oregano, and salt and pepper to taste, and simmer, stirring occasionally, until the tomatoes have reduced and separated from the oil, 15 to 20 minutes. Add the red pepper to taste, if desired, and simmer for 2 minutes more.

continued

2. While the sauce is simmering, cook the pasta in boiling salted water according to the package directions; drain.

3. Reserve all but 1 cup of the sauce. Transfer the pasta to the remaining sauce in the skillet, add the remaining 2 tablespoons of olive oil, and toss to coat. Garnish with the basil and serve with the Parmesan and reserved sauce on the side.

CARBONARA SAUCE

The recipe for this Roman dish came from Aunt Vee. Not everything we ate was Neapolitan. This sauce includes cream; the traditional pancetta and eggs sauce does not. Pancetta differs from American bacon in that it is not smoked, so if you substitute American bacon, you'll get a very different flavor. Try this recipe with pancetta cooked very slowly to eliminate the fat.

MAKES 4 TO 6 SERVINGS

1 pound pasta (preferably a long pasta, such as spaghetti, linguine, pappardelle, or fettuccine; or small to medium shells)
3 tablespoons olive oil
3 cloves garlic, smashed
¼ pound pancetta (Italian bacon), sliced thin and julienned

1 cup heavy cream
2 large egg yolks
⅓ cup freshly grated Parmesan cheese, plus additional for serving
Freshly ground black pepper

1. Bring a large saucepan of salted water to a boil. Cook the pasta according to the package directions, and drain.

2. While the pasta is cooking, make the sauce. In a large, deep skillet set over moderate heat, heat the oil until hot. Add the garlic and cook, stirring, until it's golden, about 2 minutes. Add the pancetta and cook, stirring, until it's crisp, about 3 minutes.

3. In a bowl, beat together the heavy cream and egg yolks.

4. Add the drained hot pasta to the skillet and toss to combine with the bacon. Off the heat, add the egg mixture, and gently toss to coat with the sauce. Sprinkle with the Parmesan, stirring to combine. Transfer to serving plates, season with the pepper, and serve with the additional cheese.

PROSCIUTTO SAUCE

About getting good prosciutto: It must be sliced paper thin. I know this because my mother smacked me on the back of the head if it wasn't. Of course, it was the butcher's fault, not mine, that the prosciutto was sliced too thick—but I should have been watching. Because it's so fatty, prosciutto can be difficult to handle, especially when it's very thin. So I freeze it the day before and slice it while it's still hard—much easier to work with.

MAKES 4 TO 6 SERVINGS

continued

1 tablespoon olive oil
¾ pound thinly sliced prosciutto, cut into julienne strips
4 cloves garlic, smashed
2 cups thinly sliced onions
Two 28-ounce cans plum tomatoes, including the liquid, crushed by hand or already diced

Salt and freshly ground pepper
1 pound tubular pasta, such as penne, ziti, rigatoni

1. In a large, heavy saucepan set over moderate heat, heat the olive oil until hot. Add ½ pound of the prosciutto, reserving the remaining ¼ pound for garnish, and cook it, stirring occasionally, until the fat is rendered and the prosciutto is lightly golden, about 5 minutes. Remove from the pan, leaving the fat. Add the garlic and cook, stirring, until it is golden, about 2 minutes. Add the onions and cook, stirring occasionally, until golden, 5 to 7 minutes.

2. Return the prosciutto to the pan. Add the tomatoes, tomato liquid, and salt and pepper to taste and bring to a boil. Reduce the heat to low and simmer, stirring occasionally, until the sauce is reduced and flavorful, about 1 hour.

3. Meanwhile, cook the pasta according to the package directions and drain. Return the pasta to the pan in which it was cooked, add enough of the sauce to coat the pasta and transfer to a serving dish. Sprinkle the top of the pasta with the reserved prosciutto. Transfer the remaining pasta sauce to a serving dish, and pass separately at the table.

WHITE CLAM SAUCE

In a little neighborhood, as ours was, everyone knows the butcher, the baker, the fishmonger—and they knew us. So the social contract is very powerful. Everything they sell has to be good, has to be fresh. That's one reason the food was universally of a very high quality: The household cooks had good ingredients to work with. A dish like linguine with clam sauce can be wonderful or just so-so, and the secret is merely to use good ingredients and not ruin them—that is, don't overcook, don't overseason.

MAKES 6 SERVINGS

⅔ to ¾ cup extra-virgin olive oil
8 cloves garlic, smashed
4 dozen fresh or canned littleneck clams, shucked, liquor reserved and clams chopped fine (about 3 cups)

1 cup dry white wine, such as Orvieto or Pinot Grigio
½ cup minced fresh parsley leaves
Salt and freshly ground black pepper
2 dozen littleneck clams, scrubbed
1 pound linguine or spaghettini

1. In a large saucepan set over moderate heat, heat the oil. Add the garlic and cook, stirring, until it's golden, about 2 minutes.

2. Strain the reserved clam liquor through a sieve lined with cheesecloth or through a coffee filter. Add the strained clam liquor, the wine, parsley, and salt and pepper to taste to the saucepan. Add the unshucked clams, cover the pan, and bring the liquid to a boil. Cook for 6 to 10 minutes, shaking the pan over the heat, or until the shells have opened. With a slotted spoon, transfer the clams in their shells to a bowl and reserve.

continued

3. Over moderately high heat, cook the liquid in the saucepan until it's reduced to 1 cup, or until the liquid is flavorful. Add the finely chopped clams and heat gently over moderately low heat, stirring, until just cooked, 1 to 2 minutes. Do not overcook or the clams will become tough.

4. Meanwhile, cook the pasta according to the package directions and drain.

5. Add the pasta to the sauce in the pan, toss to combine, and garnish with the reserved clams in the shells. Serve from the saucepan.

BOLOGNESE SAUCE
(Meat Sauce)

This very traditional Bolognese Sauce is obviously northern Italian in origin, but it was served in my southern Italian family. Finishing the sauce with a little heavy cream gives it a very rich flavor. Drain the pasta well and stir it into the sauce, reserving some of the sauce to serve on the side. Fresh, cold ricotta cheese is also a good accompaniment.

MAKES ABOUT 6 CUPS

½ cup olive oil

4 cloves garlic, smashed

¼ cup minced onion

¼ cup minced carrot

¼ cup minced celery

½ pound coarsely ground lean beef

½ pound ground veal

Salt and freshly ground black pepper

½ cup dry Italian red wine, such as
Chianti or Cabernet

⅛ teaspoon freshly grated nutmeg

Two 28-ounce cans crushed
tomatoes, including the juice

½ cup freshly grated Parmesan cheese

Extra-virgin olive oil or heavy cream
for finishing

Suggested pasta: penne, ziti, rigatoni,
orrechiette, fusilli

1. In a heavy saucepan set over moderate heat, heat the oil until hot. Add the garlic and cook, stirring, for 2 minutes. Add the onion and cook, stirring, until it's golden, about 3 minutes. Add the carrot and celery and cook, stirring, for 2 minutes. Add the beef, veal, and salt and pepper to taste and cook, stirring, until the meat is lightly browned, about 3 minutes. Add the wine and nutmeg and cook until the wine is completely evaporated. Add the tomatoes and bring to a boil, stirring. Simmer over very low heat, stirring occasionally, for 1½ hours. Stir in the cheese. (The sauce may be prepared 2 to 3 days ahead. Cover and chill. Freeze for up to 1 month. Defrost in the refrigerator before heating.)

2. Before serving with pasta, add a few tablespoons of extra-virgin olive oil or heavy cream, to taste, to the sauce to flavor and lightly thin it.

CAULIFLOWER AND PASTA SHELLS

Like his Pasta Puttanesca (page 76), this was another of my uncle Meade's recipes that he served to his cronies on Thanksgiving. Cauliflower is fresh and plentiful throughout the fall.

MAKES 4 TO 6 SERVINGS

4 cups Basic Marinara Sauce (page 43)
1 large head of cauliflower
1 pound small pasta shells

Salt and lots of freshly ground black pepper
¼ cup freshly grated Parmesan cheese

1. Simmer the marinara sauce in a large pot.

2. Cut the cauliflower into flowerets. Place in a large pot of salted water and bring to a boil. Reduce the heat to low and simmer until the cauliflower is tender, about 15 minutes. Drain.

3. While the cauliflower is simmering, cook the pasta according to the package directions and drain.

4. Add the cooked cauliflower to the heated marinara sauce, season with salt and pepper to taste, and simmer for 3 minutes. Pour the sauce over the pasta shells, and serve in rimmed soup bowls. Sprinkle with the Parmesan.

RAW SAUCE

There's nothing like the sweet, ripe summer tomatoes that show up in New York City markets in July and August. This uncooked sauce makes a wonderful dressing for pasta served hot or cold.

MAKES 4 TO 6 SERVINGS

2 cups diced fresh plum tomatoes, including their juice
½ cup extra-virgin olive oil
8 cloves garlic, smashed
1 cup loosely packed fresh basil leaves, sliced thin

Salt and freshly ground pepper
1 pound pasta (penne, fusilli, radiatore, or even spinach penne for the green color)
Freshly grated Parmesan cheese as an accompaniment

1. In a bowl, combine the tomatoes, oil, garlic, basil, and salt and pepper to taste, and let marinate for 2 hours.

2. Cook the pasta according to the package directions and drain. Transfer to a large bowl, add the sauce, and toss to coat. Serve with the cheese.

PASTINA FOR CHILDREN

Kids are so conservative; they want everything, always, the same: the same videos, the same stories, the same food. As children, we got the same food, with slight variations, in every home. One thing that never varied was pastina. If you were a kid and you went to someone's house, you got pastina. When my mother, who was sick for a long time before she died, went to the hospital, I was sent to my aunt Stella's house. She made pastina for me every day. It's easy to make, delicious, and kids always eat it.

MAKES 4 TO 6 SERVINGS

5 cups chicken broth
½ pound pastina or other small pasta
  for soup

2 tablespoons butter
¼ cup freshly grated Parmesan
  cheese, plus additional for serving

In a saucepan set over moderate heat, bring the chicken broth to a boil. Add the pastina and cook, stirring occasionally, until it's al dente. Stir in the butter and Parmesan and serve at once. Pass some Parmesan separately at the table.

4

THURSDAY

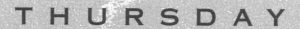

Except during warm weather, we ate soups and stews quite a bit for dinner, even more than we ate pasta. In this chapter you'll find the two heartiest soups or stews in this book, either one of which is a meal in itself.

JOE RENNY

"Y̶ou gotta earn," my father said to me. "You always gotta earn." He meant that life wasn't going to be easy, and that I would have to do something well and be productive in order to make my way in life and support a family. My father always earned. He taught his sons to earn as well. And he fulfilled the American dream of having his children do better than he did. I hope I'll be able to say the same. This is his story in his own words:

I was born in Gallatin, Pennsylvania, on the Monongahela River about eighteen miles south of Pittsburgh. My father, Attilio (Pete) Renny, grew up in Benevento, in the mountains east of Naples, and was a coal miner, so that's why he, like so many other Italians, came to the Appalachians as a teenager. My mother and father had been childhood sweethearts in Benevento, and he told my mother, Vincenza Cesare, that he would send for her when he could. They both had been born in 1886, and my mother came over when she was twenty-one, in 1907, and they were married here. My mother had two brothers who also came over, one to Schenectady and the other to Brooklyn.

My parents had seven children, of which I was the youngest. Their

The Rennys, in the summer of 1949, at Pep's the day of Joseph's christening.

Uncle Ralph and Aunt Bea entertained the soldiers in California. In uniform is their nephew Dominick (Sonny), Aunt Vee's son, on leave from the war. My father stopped by for a visit on his way back to Brooklyn after the war.

The Rennys, on Dean Street.

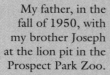

My father, in the fall of 1950, with my brother Joseph at the lion pit in the Prospect Park Zoo.

first was stillborn, then came Tony, my oldest brother, followed by Estelle. My mother then had twins who died in their first year, one after the other. Then my brother Attilio was born, and he is called Timmy. I was born September 19, 1918. I never knew my father, because he died a little more than a year later, on Columbus Day, October 12, 1919. My mother said he caught a bad cold in the mines, which turned into pneumonia; but he may also have died from the Spanish influenza that killed so many people at that time. We didn't know much then. Maybe we still don't.

So there was my mother, a widow with four children. She remarried the following year to Pasquale Ruotolo, a fruit peddler in Gallatin, and she had five children with him, first two sons, then three daughters, all of whom are still living, four of them in Ozone Park close by each other.

Pasquale also made moonshine. I used to help him, even as a little boy. I followed him up into the woods where he had his still, to keep him company. Once he sent me home to fetch an instrument he had forgot-

My confirmation, 1969. My father, in shades.

ten, something he used to test the alcohol level, like the glass tube you use to measure the antifreeze in a car radiator. I have never discussed with anyone my memories of a certain day when I was four or five years old, and the memories are a little vague. I remember sitting on the steps inside our house and looking into the kitchen, where my mother was, then seeing Don Vincenzo appear at the back door. He was holding on to the door frame with both hands and he called out to my mother, *"Vincenza, m'hanno sparato"* ("Vincenza, I've been shot").

Don Vincenzo was my stepfather's friend from Pittsburgh. He was a powerful, good-looking man in his early forties, a sharp dresser, and he had come down because a man named Chicken John wanted to muscle in on Pasquale's moonshine business. Pasquale and my brother Tony; Don Vincenzo; Chicken John; and his son, a young man around twenty, were in the backyard playing cards and drinking. Suddenly, there was shooting. In the house, I heard the sound of gunfire—*pop, pop, pop*—but I didn't see anything. Pasquale grabbed Tony, and they hid behind a wall. Chicken John's son was also shot, and the father and son ran off. The son's body was later found near a coal mine about a mile away. There was a trial, and Chicken John went to jail.

In 1927, when I was eight years old, my mother's four nephews came from Brooklyn and spent the whole summer with us. When summer was over, my stepfather went back with them to Brooklyn where he stayed on and found work as a laborer in the building line. Perhaps he thought he was safer from the vengeance of Chicken John, who had threatened to kill him. A year later, he sent for his family.

Island Park. My father is second from the right, with his arm around his sister.

We weren't in Brooklyn long before the stock market crash came, followed by the Depression. My stepfather couldn't get work; nobody could. Nobody ate. He was working for the WPA in 1935 when he fell off a truck and hit his head; he never came to, and ten days later he died, so my mother was widowed again at age forty-nine. Don Vincenzo came from Pittsburgh to pay his respects. That year I finished up my first year of high school and joined the Civil Conservation Corps. I stayed in it for four years. I was a dollar-a-day man. Every month $22 was sent home to my mother, and I got $8 to take care of incidentals.

The CCC was good. It kept a lot of us young guys off the streets and out of trouble, and it prepared us for the war. I went to upstate New York, but I also went to the Northwest. One June we were sent up to Warm Lake, Idaho, which is 8,000 feet high, so even in summer we were knee deep in snow. We had to be back down to Gallagher by October or we'd be snowed in. And on the other side of the mountain was Sun Valley, which in the '30s was where all the celebrities from Hollywood came—Clark Gable and Carole Lombard, all those people. But we never saw any of them.

I came back to Brooklyn in 1939 and worked as a driver for a trucking company in the garment district. The following year my mother died, age fifty-four, same age as Gerard's mother when she died. I became the sole support of my three younger half-sisters, who were ten, twelve, and fourteen. We moved in with my older sister, Estelle, who had married in 1937, and I went to work as a welder in the Brooklyn Navy Yard.

I had known Jennie Manfellotti since we were children. Both families knew each other. While I was working at the navy yard, I asked her one night if she wanted to go bowling with me. She got all excited because she got a strike and she started hugging me. That's when we started to get serious.

When the war broke out, I should have been classified 2B as an essential war worker; the head of the navy yard said I was needed. But the local draft commissioner had it in for Italians. He really made me mad in the interview. He said, "Don't you want to fight for your country? Or would you rather fight for Mussolini and Italy?" I went to the National Board in Manhattan and the guy there agreed with me—after all, I had four brothers in the service—and he told me to get classified or I'd find myself in the army. That's when I got classified 3A for dependency deferral, since my three younger half sisters were all dependent on me. But my younger sisters were considered part of Estelle's household because they were living with her and her husband, so I was reclassified 1A and drafted in June of 1942.

I entered the Army Air Force and did my basic training at Miami Beach. At that time Fort Lauderdale was really a fort—a gunnery range in the sand dunes. I

A neighborhood reunion at Fort Dix during World War II.

came back up to Brooklyn in October of 1943, and Jennie and I were married on the tenth. A few weeks later, she came down to Hapeville, Georgia, and lived with me off the base. But in January of 1944 I shipped out and Jennie went home. She had gotten pregnant, but I didn't know it at the time. My oldest son, Attilio, also called Timmy, was born in August of 1944.

I joined a B-29 squadron as a refueler and was stationed first in Calcutta, then in Tinian, one of the Mariana Islands, rear bases for the B-29 missions to bomb Japan.

In July of 1945, another squadron arrived in Tinian; but it was fenced off from the others in the group. The soldiers were just ordinary soldiers, but they wouldn't even talk to us. It was all top secret. I didn't know it then, but the *Enola Gay* was behind that fence. On August 8, one plane departed for Hiroshima. Two days later another plane departed for Nagasaki. We knew then what all the secrecy was about. But the Japanese didn't surrender right away, so on August 14 all of the planes in all four squadrons were sent out to bomb Japan. We called that mission "The Inducer," because it convinced Japan to surrender.

I was sent back home on Columbus Day and discharged in Sacramento, California. From there I went to San Pedro, in Southern California, where I stayed eight days with Jennie's uncle Ralph. He told her he wasn't going to let me go home and she was going to have to move west to join me. I wonder what would have happened if I had stayed in California. I suppose it would have been different.

I saw my son for the first time when he was fourteen months old. They had waited for me to come back before Timmy got his first haircut. Jennie gave me a lock of his hair from that first haircut, and I carried it around for years. I had started the war a single man; I came back home married and a father.

Timmy, in the pram, seeing our father for the first time. My mother waited for my father to come home from the war so he could take Timmy for his first haircut. My father kept a lock of Timmy's hair wrapped in cellophane in his wallet until 1997, when he decided to give it to Timmy.

I didn't qualify for the usual severance pay for servicemen, which was $20 for fifty-two weeks, because my job in the navy yard was supposedly waiting for me. But that job didn't look very secure—the shipyards were laying men off—so I went back to driving. For two years I drove a truck for the Moscarella & Sons winery on Hester Street. One of the sons was a talent manager, and through him I met an eighteen-year-old singer named Tony Bennett. In 1947, I started driving a truck for Times Square Stores, and I did that for twenty-two years. From 1969 to 1980, I drove a New York City bus.

My second son, Joseph, was born in 1949. Jennie and I had a daughter, Nancy, who was born in March of 1957, but she died in December of that same year. Gerard was born in 1959. Two years later Jennie had her first open-heart surgery. The medical expenses were high and I was making less than $100 a week as a driver, so I started bookmaking then. I never got rich, but I made a few extra bucks. I was working, so I was never home during the day. My customers and I were very discreet; they called me in the evening. The cops were around during the day, so they never caught on. I also made extra money bringing cigarettes back from North Carolina. It was a twelve-hour drive each way; but I could haul 2,000 cartons in one trip. They sold for $1.90 a carton in North Carolina; I could sell them for nearly double that amount and they were still cheaper than in New York City, so I had a lot of customers. One day the cops came by when I wasn't home and knocked on the door looking for me. My wife asked what they wanted. They didn't have a search warrant, so they said they wanted to buy some cigarettes. My wife said

The Rennys at the American Legion Hall, in October 1958. All three sons are present because my mother is pregnant with me.

they had the wrong place. She called our upstairs neighbors, who came over and, with Gerard, who was home then, brought the boxes of cigarettes upstairs to their apartment, just to be on the safe side. With the cops sitting around outside the apartment, I sent Gerard around to make deliveries in his big winter coat stuffed with cigarettes.

When the veterans came back to the neighborhood, we started an American Legion post on Eastern Parkway, between Dean and Pacific. It was the Marrotta-Yanotta Post, named for two boys from the neighborhood who were killed in the war. We had 200-some-odd members north, east, south, and west of there, from six or seven square blocks around—from Fulton Street and Ocean Hill and Brownsville. In the early '50s we held a dance for about 800 people. We rented out the Knights of Columbus Hall in Grand Army Plaza. We held dinner dances through the '50s, and we had about ten years of good activity, then it petered out in the '60s.

I joined a social club in the 1960s. It was called the Imbriani Society, and it was an old organization for Italian-American veterans from World War I. A lot of the older men were starting to pass away, so they took all the younger Italian guys. It was at Dean and Stone Streets, across from Pep's. We would hold a dinner and dance about once a year, usually in October or November.

From 1954 on, I was involved in the Holy Name Society, which was affiliated with Our Lady of Loreto. Father Anthony Barretta was a terrific organizer. He got everybody in the neighborhood to donate labor and materials, and we converted an old garage across from the church into the Don Bosco Center. Every month, some of us in the Holy Name Society bought raffle tickets to sell for the church. I'd buy three books of ten tickets each and try to sell the tickets for a dollar apiece, and I used to eat what I couldn't sell. We were the 50-50 Club: The church got 50 percent of what we sold, and the winners of the raffle got 50 percent. We raised a lot of money for the church every month. We used to call Father Barretta "the hoodlum priest" because he had everybody in the neighborhood working for the church. He got the racketeers to donate stuff, he had bookmakers working for him.

In addition to the dinner dances the Holy Name held twice a year, we also had

Father Barretta and the Lady of Loreto women's bowling team. My mother is sixth from the left.

a street carnival, in late spring and early fall, which we set up in Pacific Street and in the churchyard. We had all the usual rides and games, and I used to run the dice cage. When the guys came around selling raffle tickets, I always bought two or three and put Gerard's name on them. On the last night of the carnival, they'd have the drawing, and one year Gerard won $1,500. He must have been about three and a half. He was my good luck charm—he still is. Unfortunately, I invested the money in a gas station in the neighborhood just as the neighborhood was going down, and I had to let it go the following year.

My wife belonged to the Altar Rosary Society, which was the women's auxiliary of the Holy Name Society. She loved bowling so much they made her president of the bowling team, and she went bowling one night a week from October to May. The men had their own bowling team, and we went bowling a different night of the week.

Our neighborhood in East New York was a great place to grow up and to raise a family. But it started to change in the 1960s. The younger people who were moving up in the world didn't stay. So there were fewer and fewer Italian families, and the old people were retiring or dying off, and a lot of the businesses were closing. And when the neighborhood stopped being primarily Italian, it changed from the place where every grandparent knew everyone else's grandchildren. It just wasn't the same. So when Gerard was ten, I moved the family to Long Island, which is where I live today with my second wife, Lenora. We have a good life. I started life as a coal miner's son, I went around the world, I served my country, I raised my three sons. I've got no regrets.

RED BEEF SOUP

Italians eat soup more than they eat pasta. My father eats like a peasant—give him a bowl of soup and some good bread and he's happy. Happiness always seems to come from the simplest things.

MAKES 4 TO 6 SERVINGS

3 tablespoons olive oil
2½ to 3 pounds beef neck bones
2 carrots, sliced
2 celery stalks, sliced
1 onion, sliced
2 cloves garlic, minced

7 cups water or beef broth
Salt and freshly ground black pepper
1 cup tubetti or similar small pasta
Freshly grated Parmesan cheese as an
    accompaniment

1. In a large saucepan or casserole set over moderate heat, heat the oil until hot. Add the beef and cook, turning, until it's browned, 5 to 7 minutes. Transfer the beef to a plate.

2. Add the carrots, celery, onion, and garlic to the saucepan or casserole and cook, stirring frequently, until the onion is golden, about 5 minutes. Add the water or broth and salt and pepper to taste and bring to a boil. Reduce the heat to low and simmer, skimming and stirring occasionally, until the meat is tender, 1 to 1½ hours.

3. Stir in the tubetti and simmer, 5 to 7 minutes, stirring occasionally, until tender. Serve the soup with the Parmesan.

MACARONI PIE

Buster is my brother Timmy's friend from the Cadets, the neighborhood drum and bugle corps. When I first started talking about this cookbook, everyone said, "You've gotta get Buster's recipe for Macaroni Pie." It's always a hit at the club. This simple dinner is more about shopping than cooking. Get your grocer to slice the sausage or pepperoni and grate the cheese for you. Combine the ingredients, cook the pasta, bake—dinner is ready in less than an hour.

MAKES 8 SERVINGS

1 pound linguine
½ pound dry Italian sausage or
   pepperoni, sweet or hot, sliced thin
12 large eggs

1 cup milk
1 cup freshly grated Parmesan cheese
Salt and freshly ground pepper

1. Preheat the oven to 350°F. Oil a 9-by-13-by-2-inch baking pan.

2. Bring a large pot of salted water to a boil. Cook the linguine until al dente and drain.

3. In a large bowl, combine the pasta with the sausage, and transfer to the baking pan.

4. In a bowl, whisk together the eggs, milk, ¾ cup of the cheese, and salt and pepper to taste, and pour the mixture over the pasta. Sprinkle the top with the remaining cheese.

5. Bake the pie for 20 to 25 minutes, or until the eggs are set. If desired, run under a preheated broiler about 4 inches from the heat until the top is golden.

COYOTE CHICKEN
Roast Chicken Hunter's Style

I don't think this dish had a name in our household; it was just roast chicken. It was when I was visiting my cousins that I heard it called Coyote Chicken. My guess is that my uncle named it that because it was also called "hunter's style" chicken—and what kind of hunter hunts chickens? A coyote, right? Besides, the word for hunter in Italian (*cacciatore*) looks a little like "coyote." The defining ingredient in this dish is the canned peas. Any good cook knows that canned peas are an entirely different vegetable from fresh or frozen peas, and the liquid in the can is as essential as the peas themselves. The chicken should be cut in small pieces so they will cook through without becoming dry. The peas go on top, and the juice mixes with the other ingredients to make a delicious broth to be sopped up with bread. My mother also made this as a Sunday company dish in addition to the Sunday gravy.

MAKES 4 SERVINGS

One 3- to 3½-pound chicken, cut into 10 pieces, rinsed and patted dry

1 onion, sliced thin

10 to 12 cloves garlic, smashed, or to taste

½ cup olive oil

3 to 4 tablespoons fresh lemon juice, or to taste

Salt and freshly ground black pepper

2 medium to large Idaho or Russet potatoes (about 1 pound), peeled and cut into 1-inch cubes

Two 15-ounce cans LeSueur peas, including liquid

continued

1. In a shallow dish, combine the chicken, onion, and garlic. In a small bowl, whisk together the olive oil, lemon juice, and salt and pepper to taste and pour over the chicken, turning to coat with the oil. Let marinate, covered and chilled, for 30 minutes to 2 hours.

2. Preheat the oven to 375°F. In a large, shallow roasting pan, arrange the chicken mixture along with the potatoes in a single layer, and bake for 45 minutes, turning frequently, until the juices run clear.

3. Add the peas together with the liquid to the pan, and place under a preheated broiler 3 to 4 inches from the heat, until the chicken and potatoes are golden brown and the peas are heated through.

4. Transfer the chicken to soup plates and spoon the vegetables and liquid over it.

JOE RENNY'S BEEF STEW

This is another of my father's recipes, which, like the Steak Pizzaiola (page 22), includes Worcestershire sauce. And also like Steak Pizzaiola, his beef stew was his way of making dinner an important tradition in his family.

MAKES 6 SERVINGS

1½ pounds beef stew meat, such as chuck, cut into 1½-inch pieces

Salt and freshly ground black pepper

4 tablespoons olive oil

Worcestershire sauce to taste

1 onion, sliced

2 cloves garlic, smashed

3 cups water or beef broth

1 bay leaf

1 teaspoon dried thyme, crumbled

½ pound baby carrots, cut into 1½-inch pieces

2 stalks celery, cut into 1½-inch pieces

4 medium to large red potatoes (about 1½ pounds), peeled and cut into 1½-inch pieces

One 15-ounce can LeSueur peas, drained

1. Pat the meat dry and season with the salt and pepper.

2. In a large saucepan or casserole set over moderately high heat, heat 3 tablespoons of the olive oil until hot. Add the meat and Worcestershire sauce and cook, turning, until the meat is browned, 3 to 4 minutes. Transfer the meat to a plate.

3. Add the remaining tablespoon of oil to the pan and the onion and garlic and cook, over moderate heat, stirring occasionally, until golden, about 7 minutes. Add the water or broth, bay leaf, thyme, carrots, celery, potatoes, and salt and pepper to taste and bring to a boil. Skim the stew, reduce the heat to low, and simmer, partially covered, stirring occasionally, until the meat is tender, about 1 hour. During the last 5 minutes of cooking, add the peas.

5

FRIDAY

When I was growing up, the Catholic Church still required that no one eat meat on Friday. Unfortunately for me, I hated fish. And I wasn't the only one. There was lots of cheese pizza consumed in my neighborhood on Friday nights. Fish was inescapable, however, on Christmas Eve, and I have included some seafood and fish recipes in the Christmas chapter.

A hayride in the 1950s. The organizer, Al Ciullo, is seated in the center.

Al Ciullo as a young boxer. His managers were Hap Maione
and Frank "the Dasher" Abbondando.

Graduation from Loreto, 1969.

At Al and Frieda's house. *From left*: Joe Naso, Frieda, Katherine Naso, Al, and Kid Gap.

Men at the wedding of Anthony Corozzo's godfather, Ernie Romano, at the Premier Palace in 1946. At the far left is John "Jazzi" Cesare; at the far right is Anthony's uncle Allie Corozzo; to Allie's left is Jimmy "Blabber" Esposito. In the back row are the groom's brother, Anthony "Wolf" Romano, *left*, and Pasqual Ciccarelli, *right*.

LENTIL SOUP

This soup is completely vegetarian. It was considered good luck to eat lentils on New Year's Eve or New Year's Day; but we ate them all year round.

MAKES ABOUT 8 CUPS, OR 4 TO 6 SERVINGS

¼ cup olive oil
2 carrots, sliced
1 stalk celery, sliced
1 onion, sliced
2 cups lentils, rinsed and picked over

One 1-pound can tomatoes, drained and chopped; or 1 cup diced fresh plum tomatoes
8 cups water
Salt and freshly ground black pepper

In a large saucepan or casserole set over moderate heat, heat the oil until hot. Cook the carrots, celery, and onion in the oil, stirring occasionally, for 5 minutes. Add the lentils, tomatoes, water, and salt and pepper to taste and simmer the soup, skimming and stirring occasionally, for 30 minutes, or until the lentils are tender.

SPAGHETTINI AGLIO E OLIO
Thin Spaghetti with Garlic and Olive Oil

Some of the best Italian dishes are the simplest. For this classic bachelor's dish, use good olive oil and don't overdo the parsley—it's mainly for color. Spaghettini is, of course, a thinner version of spaghetti. The general rule with pasta is: The heavier the sauce, the thicker the pasta. Garlic and oil sauce is so light, it demands a thin pasta.

MAKES 4 TO 6 SERVINGS

1 pound spaghettini or similar pasta
½ cup extra-virgin olive oil
6 to 8 cloves garlic, smashed

1 tablespoon minced fresh parsley leaves
Red pepper flakes (optional)
Salt

1. Cook the pasta according to the package directions.

2. Meanwhile, make the sauce. In a large skillet set over moderately high heat, heat the oil until hot. Add the garlic and cook, stirring, until it's golden, 30 to 60 seconds. Add the parsley, red pepper flakes to taste, if using, and salt to taste, and cook, stirring, for 1 minute. Remove the pan from the heat.

3. Drain the pasta and transfer it to the skillet. Set the skillet over moderately low heat. Toss the pasta until it's well coated with the sauce, and correct the seasoning, adding more salt and red pepper flakes to taste.

PASTA PUTTANESCA
Spaghetti, Whore's Style

This style of pasta was a specialty of Neapolitan working girls who whipped up a little nutrition between assignments. We have two versions here: one by my uncle Meade, Brooklyn chairman of the Democratic party, who traditionally served this dish to the movers and shakers of New York on Thanksgiving (was he commenting on the nature of politics?); the other, a variation I concocted that has become a new Christmas Eve tradition in our household.

GERARD RENNY VERSION
(WITH TOMATO SAUCE)
MAKES 4 TO 6 SERVINGS

½ cup olive oil

7 cloves garlic

One 2-ounce can anchovy fillets, drained

One 28-ounce can crushed tomatoes with puree

One 28-ounce can plum tomatoes, including the liquid, chopped coarse

1 cup Kalamata olives, pitted and minced

½ cup Gaeta or green olives, pitted and minced

One 3-ounce jar capers, drained

½ teaspoon dried red pepper flakes, or to taste (optional)

Freshly ground black pepper

1 pound spaghettini, linguine or other thin-strand pasta

1. In a blender, combine all but 3 tablespoons of the oil, the garlic, and anchovies and blend until smooth.

2. In a heavy saucepan set over moderate heat, add the anchovy mixture and cook, stirring, for 2 minutes. Add all the tomatoes and bring to a boil, then add the olives, capers, red pepper flakes, if using, and pepper to taste. Reduce the heat to low and simmer, stirring occasionally, for 1 to 1½ hours, until the sauce darkens.

3. Meanwhile, cook the pasta according to package directions and drain. Return the pasta to the pan in which it was cooked, add enough sauce to coat along with the remaining 3 tablespoons of olive oil, and transfer to a serving dish. Serve the remaining sauce separately.

UNCLE MEADE'S VERSION
(WITHOUT TOMATO SAUCE)
MAKES 4 TO 6 SERVINGS

½ cup olive oil

2 cloves garlic, minced

4 anchovy fillets, chopped

3 tablespoons finely chopped fresh parsley

3 pitted Gaeta olives, sliced

1 teaspoon capers, drained

Lots of freshly ground black pepper

1 pound spaghettini, linguine, or other thin-strand pasta

1. In a skillet over medium heat, heat the oil and cook the garlic, stirring, until it's soft, about 2 minutes. Add the chopped anchovies to the skillet. When the anchovies have disintegrated, add half the parsley, the olives, capers, and pepper to taste. Simmer for a few minutes.

2. Remove the sauce from the heat, and pour over hot pasta. Sprinkle with the remaining parsley.

continued

POTATOES AND EGGS

Like Spaghettini Aglio e Olio (page 75), Potatoes and Eggs is a classic bachelor's dish—easy to make, satisfying, and you probably have the ingredients in your kitchen. Andy, the club's most frequent chef, made this dish at the club every Thursday night, so I started making it again because I was reminded of my mother. She made this especially for me on Friday, or she made it for everyone on Saturday because she had spent the entire day cooking for Sunday. Now we have it at my house for Sunday brunch. To make it even simpler, I'll order extra home fries the night before, if my wife and I have gone out to dinner at a steak house. I cook the home fries in the morning (until they're a little crunchy) and skip step 1. In this version, you end up with a frittata, which is nice. On the other hand, it tastes just as good if you end up with something more free-form.

MAKES 4 SERVINGS AS AN ENTRÉE,
6 AS A SIDE DISH

2 large red or new potatoes (about 1 pound)
4 to 5 tablespoons olive oil, or to taste
Salt and freshly ground black pepper
5 large eggs
½ cup milk

1 cup grated Romano cheese, plus additional for sprinkling
3 tablespoons minced fresh parsley leaves
½ to 1 teaspoon dried red pepper flakes, or to taste

1. Peel the potatoes and cut into pieces resembling French fries. Pat dry.

2. In an oven-safe 10-inch skillet set over moderately high heat, heat the oil until

hot. Add the potatoes and salt and pepper to taste and cook, turning occasionally, until the potatoes are browned and crisp, 5 to 7 minutes.

3. Meanwhile, in a bowl, beat together the eggs, milk, ¾ cup of the Romano cheese, the parsley, red pepper flakes, and salt to taste.

4. Add the eggs to the skillet and cook over moderate heat, gently stirring, until the eggs are golden brown and just set on the underside, 2 to 3 minutes.

5. Sprinkle the top of the potatoes and eggs with the remaining ¼ cup of grated Romano and place under a preheated broiler about 3 to 4 inches from the heat for 2 to 4 minutes, or until the cheese bubbles and browns. Transfer to a serving plate and serve cut into wedges.

EGGPLANT PARMIGIANA

This vegetarian casserole makes a truly satisfying meal. Leftovers reheated the following day are even better.

1 large (1¼ to 1½ pounds) eggplant, trimmed and cut into ¼-inch-thick slices
All-purpose flour for dredging
2 large eggs
½ cup freshly grated Parmesan cheese
Salt and freshly ground black pepper
¼ cup olive oil
3 cups Basic Marinara Sauce (page 43)
½ pound mozzarella, sliced

1. Preheat the oven to 350°F. Oil a shallow baking dish.

2. Dredge the eggplant slices in the flour, shaking off the excess. In a bowl, whisk together the eggs and 2 tablespoons of the Parmesan. Dip the eggplant slices in the egg and dredge again in the flour. Season with salt and pepper to taste.

3. In a large skillet set over moderately high heat, heat the oil until hot. Add the eggplant slices and fry them, in batches, until golden brown on each side, 2 to 3 minutes on the first side and 1 to 2 minutes on the second side. Drain on paper towels.

4. Transfer the eggplant to the baking dish, top with some of the sauce, and cover with the mozzarella. Drizzle with the remaining sauce and sprinkle with the remaining Parmesan. Bake for 30 minutes, or until golden.

ESCAROLE AND BEANS

With escarole you should take care to divide the leaves between the thicker, heavier ones and the more tender ones, and then cook the former first for a few minutes longer in order to have an even texture.

MAKES 6 SERVINGS

2 heads escarole
¼ cup olive oil
8 large cloves garlic, smashed
½ teaspoon dried red pepper flakes,
    or to taste
Salt

1 cup water
Two 19-ounce cans cannellini beans,
    including liquid
¼ pound prosciutto, thinly sliced and
    julienned

1. Trim the ends of the escarole, halve each, and rinse well in 3 changes of water. Drain in a colander.

2. In a casserole set over moderate heat, warm the oil until it's hot. Cook the garlic, stirring, until it's golden, about 2 minutes. Add the escarole, red pepper, and salt to taste and cook, covered, turning frequently, for about 10 minutes. Add the water and bring to a boil. Reduce the heat to low and simmer, covered, stirring occasionally, for 10 minutes more. Add the beans and liquid and the prosciutto and cook, uncovered, stirring occasionally, until the escarole is tender, about 10 minutes.

3. Transfer to a bowl and serve with Italian bread and a sprinkling of Parmesan cheese.

Friday night out with the guys. Second from the left is my uncle Al Ciullo, who's married to my mother's sister Frieda. Al was a live wire, always getting people together, getting them to go out for the evening. He loved going to cabarets, where girls with cameras photographed the patrons at special events. The photos were sent in souvenir folders.

Saturday night at Club 82, at 82 East 4 Street in Manhattan. That's my mother at the far left and her sister Frieda at the far right. My father is second from the right, and Al Ciullo, Frieda's husband, is fourth from the right. Friday night was guys' night out, and some of those guys had a *goomata* (girlfriend) whom the wives didn't know about. So Saturday night was always a night out with the wives and it was sacrosanct. Years later, I bought this place and re-opened it as a rock 'n' roll club with Ron Wood of the Rolling Stones. It was called Woody's in the Village.

6

SATURDAY

On Saturdays, the women in the neighborhood spent all day preparing the Sunday gravy, so it was customary to eat light. Since children were not in school, they were running in and out of the house and nibbling all day rather than having a big meal at dinnertime. Summertime was best of all—kids' day every day—and this chapter includes a number of good warm-weather recipes.

On the corner in front of Pep's. Felicia is seated, *center*, flanked by her cousin, *left*, and my brother Joseph and cousin Vivienne.

A neighborhood gathering in Highland Park off Jamaica Avenue. I'm not sure what the occasion was. People in the neighborhood didn't need much of an excuse to get together and get out and enjoy a nice day. In the lower left are my brothers Timmy and Joseph—part of a tightly knit neighborhood.

Sandlots forever. In the 1940s, the Dodgers still ruled in Brooklyn and the boys in the neighborhood idolized them.

Poor neighborhoods seem to produce good boxers. This picture shows one of a dozen or so boxing clubs in East New York. Front row center is my uncle Al Ciullo. Al was sort of a posterboy for the "knockaround guy." He would work, occasionally, but mostly he was working some angle with an eye out for a fast buck. At one time, he and his twin brother, Jimmy, ran a barbershop. Jimmy did most of the haircutting, and there wasn't much of that. Mainly, the barbershop was a place to hang out. The boxing clubs, too, were hangouts, although they did produce some contenders.

Young couples ready for a Saturday night on the town.

Young couple in Callahan-Kelly Park on Eastern Parkway.

Just hanging out. Anthony Corozzo, second from the right, and friends.

PASTA E FAGIOLI
Pasta and Beans

This is another of my uncle Meade's recipes. The pasta he preferred is ditalini, "little thimbles," but any chunky pasta will do. You can prepare this dish with one 3-quart saucepan.

MAKES FIVE 12-OUNCE SERVINGS

½ cup ditalini (more if desired)

2 tablespoons olive oil

3 cloves garlic, minced

½ cup celery leaves, chopped

1 celery stalk, diced (about ½ cup)

¼ pound prosciutto, thinly sliced and julienned

One 14½-ounce can peeled Italian plum tomatoes, diced

Two 15-ounce cans cannellini beans, with liquid

2 cups water

Freshly ground black pepper

1. Fill a 3-quart saucepan with water and bring to a boil. Add the ditalini and cook less than al dente, 9 or 10 minutes. Drain in a colander, rinse with cold water, and set aside.

2. In the same saucepan, heat the oil over moderate heat and add the garlic, celery (leaves and stalk), and prosciutto. Cook over medium-low heat, stirring occasionally, until the celery is a little soft, about 7 minutes. Stir in the tomatoes and simmer for a minute or two. Blend in the undrained beans, water, and pepper to taste. Raise the heat to high and bring to a boil; then reduce the heat to a low boil and cook until the mixture thickens, 35 to 40 minutes.

3. Blend in the ditalini, simmer for 15 minutes, and serve.

FRIED PEPPER "WET" SANDWICH

Like the other sandwiches in this book, this was made for us in the kitchen of Pep's restaurant. My father made this for himself when he was just looking for something to eat—nothing fancy, just very satisfying. You really have to be patient and let the peppers cool before eating them or the oils can burn your mouth. Your patience is rewarded with great taste. Also, do not use bell peppers for this recipe. Italian peppers are not hot, and are pale green in color.

MAKES 4 SERVINGS

⅓ cup olive oil
6 large Italian frying peppers,
    stemmed and seeded, but left
    whole

Salt and freshly ground black pepper
Extra-virgin olive oil to taste
    (optional)
One 14- to 16-inch loaf Italian bread

1. In a large, deep skillet set over moderate heat, heat the oil. Add the peppers and salt and pepper to taste, and fry, turning frequently, until the peppers are browned and soft. As the peppers soften, gently crush them into the oil with the back of a large spoon and continue to fry until they're very soft, 6 to 8 minutes. Transfer the peppers to a bowl and let them cool to room temperature. Season with additional salt and pepper and, if desired, drizzle with the extra-virgin olive oil.

2. Split the Italian loaf in half lengthwise leaving one side hinged, and remove some of the inner crumb.

3. Spoon the peppers with some of their liquid onto the Italian loaf and cut into 4 sandwiches.

HAM AND SWISS SANDWICH WITH MARINATED TOMATOES

These hearty ham and Swiss sandwiches are great for summertime, when beefsteak tomatoes are ripe and flavorful. The tomato juice blends with the marinade to make a delicious and spicy condiment for the sandwich. If you can find good hothouse tomatoes in January, you can also serve this on Super Bowl Sunday.

MAKES 6 SERVINGS

FOR THE MARINADE

¼ cup extra-virgin olive oil
⅛ cup white vinegar
Salt and freshly ground black pepper

TO CONTINUE

2 large beefsteak tomatoes, cut into
    ¼-inch slices
Two 18-inch loaves Italian bread
½ pound Swiss cheese, sliced paper
    thin
1 pound ham, sliced tissue-paper thin

1. In a small bowl, combine the ingredients for the marinade. In a shallow dish such as a pie pan or baking dish, pour the marinade over the tomatoes. Allow them to marinate for 10 to 15 minutes.

2. Split the Italian loaves in half lengthwise leaving one side hinged. Remove some of the inner crumb.

continued

3. Spoon or pour the marinade over both sides of the open loaves and make a layer of tomato slices on each loaf. Make another layer of Swiss cheese slices on top of the tomatoes. Top the cheese with a layer of ham piled loosely. Fold the 2 halves of the loaves together and cut into 6-inch slices.

STRINGBEAN SALAD

Another great summertime side dish. In Italy, vegetables are often lightly cooked, tossed with a little oil, and served room temperature. Today I would use the thin French beans, *haricots verts,* for this dish. At home we used garden variety green beans, which need a little longer to cook.

MAKES 4 SERVINGS

1 pound green beans, trimmed and
  cut in half
1 clove garlic, minced, or to taste
¼ cup extra-virgin olive oil

Salt and freshly ground black pepper
2 tablespoons fresh lemon juice
  (optional)

1. Bring a saucepan of salted water to a boil. Cook the beans for 7 minutes, or until al dente. Drain and refresh under cold water. Pat dry.

2. While the beans are cooking, make the dressing. In a serving bowl, whisk together the garlic, olive oil, and salt and pepper to taste.

3. Transfer the drained beans to the bowl with the dressing and toss to coat. Before serving, season with the lemon juice, if desired.

PICKLED EGGPLANT

Every summer my father's sister, my aunt Virginia, must have had a bumper crop of eggplant, because she made enormous quantities of this dish and passed it around the neighborhood. She still does—only she has farther to send her jars now that we're scattered all over the region.

MAKES ABOUT 4 CUPS

1 large (1¼ to 1½ pounds) eggplant
1 quart white vinegar
½ cup extra-virgin olive oil
4 cloves garlic, minced

½ teaspoon dried red pepper flakes
1½ teaspoons minced fresh oregano,
    or ½ teaspoon dried, crumbled
Salt

continued

1. Trim the eggplant and cut it in half crosswise. Cut each half lengthwise into ½-inch-thick slices. Cut the slices into ¼-inch-thick strips—similar to French fries.

2. In a shallow dish, spread the eggplant strips into layers, cover with 2 cups of the vinegar, and weight with a plate to submerge the eggplant. Let marinate for 30 minutes. Drain the eggplant and gently squeeze out the excess liquid. Repeat the same process, covering with vinegar, weighting, and marinating for 30 minutes. Squeeze out the excess liquid.

3. Meanwhile, in a bowl, whisk together the oil, garlic, red pepper, oregano, and salt to taste.

4. Transfer the eggplant strips to a 1-quart sterilized jar, and add the olive oil mixture, being sure to completely cover the eggplant and adding more oil if necessary. Let marinate, tightly covered with a lid, in a cool, dry place for 1 day.

5. Serve as an appetizer, in salads, or on sandwiches. The eggplant can be stored in sterilized jars for up to a week.

7

S U N D A Y

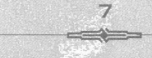

Sunday was our weekly feast day. We had our rituals of going to church, picking up our pastries, sitting down for the Sunday dinner at around two o'clock in the afternoon, and eating for hours.

The Esposito clan at Pep's. Pep himself is seated, *center*, with his son, Meade, over his right shoulder and Meade's favorite niece, my mother, over Pep's left shoulder. Pep's wife, Felicia, is seated to Pep's left. Some of the main contributors to this cookbook are shown here: on Felicia's left is Aunt Josie, and to her left is her daughter, my cousin Connie; behind Connie is my grandmother, Mary; far left, standing, is Aunt Gracie; third from left, seated, is Aunt Vee.

In the back center is Josie's husband, Augie (or Wisty), who died in 1972. My uncle Ralph came back to Brooklyn from California after the funeral, which was on a Saturday night, and he died there the following day. Aunt Vee's son Dominic, known as Sonny, escorted his uncle's body back to California. My great-grandmother Felicia died a year later, in July 1973.

Grandmother Mary Manfellotti holding Joseph; brother Timmy with cousin
Angela.

Older men on a winter day at the corner of Herkimer and Monaco.

Women of the Esposito clan.

Wedding at Our Lady of Loreto. A lot of the people in the photo are neighbors who just showed up.

Timmy and Ticia's wedding, 1973. At the far right is Harold Fischer, head of the Metropolitan Transit Authority, who dined at Pep's every Sunday.

Anthony's father, Rocco, being confirmed at Loreto in the 1930s.

SUNDAY GRAVY

MAKES 10 CUPS, DRAINED OF MEAT

2½ to 3 pounds spareribs, separated into ribs, or short ribs

⅓ cup olive oil, plus extra for tossing

2 onions, minced

12 cloves garlic, smashed

1 recipe Braciole (page 100)

1 pound Italian sausage (optional)

Four 28-ounce cans peeled plum tomatoes, including the liquid

¼ cup minced fresh oregano leaves; or 2 teaspoons dried, crumbled

¼ cup minced fresh parsley leaves; or 2 teaspoons dried, crumbled

2 bay leaves

2 teaspoons salt

1 teaspoon freshly ground black pepper

1 recipe Meatballs (recipe follows)

1 pound pasta, such as spaghetti, penne, or rigatoni, per 2 cups of sauce

1. In a casserole or stockpot, combine the ribs with enough cold water to cover by 2 inches. Bring to a boil and simmer for 20 minutes. Drain.

2. In a 10-quart casserole set over moderate heat, warm the oil and cook the onions and garlic, stirring frequently, for 5 minutes. Add the ribs, braciole, and sausage and cook until they're browned, 6 to 8 minutes. Add the tomatoes, herbs, and salt and pepper. Bring the mixture to a boil. Reduce the heat to low and simmer, stirring occasionally, for 1 hour. Add the meatballs and cook for 1 to 1½ hours more. The longer the cooking time, the more concentrated the gravy will be.

3. When the gravy is almost done, cook the pasta according to the package directions, until al dente. Drain.

4. Remove all of the meat from the sauce and put on a platter. Pour some of the sauce into a gravy boat to serve on the side. (See note below.) Add the pasta to the remaining sauce and toss with a little oil.

NOTE: The ingredients can be halved for a smaller yield. However, the sauce freezes well and can be used as a base for Braciole.

MEATBALLS

The Sunday Gravy was prepared the day before, with braciole and meatballs. Some people put raisins or pine nuts in their meatballs. My mother also made extra, otherwise she wouldn't have had any for the Sunday Gravy, because we would have eaten them all on Saturday.

MAKES 6 TO 8 SERVINGS

1 cup cubed stale bread (as from an
    Italian loaf)
Milk for soaking the bread
1 pound lean ground beef, such as
    sirloin
3 cloves garlic, minced
½ cup minced fresh parsley leaves
½ cup freshly grated Romano cheese

2 large eggs
Salt and freshly ground black pepper
3 tablespoons olive oil
4 cups Basic Marinara Sauce
    (page 43)
2 pounds cooked pasta
Freshly grated Parmesan cheese for
    serving

continued

1. In a small bowl, combine the bread with enough milk to just cover and let the bread soak for 10 minutes. Squeeze dry and chop fine.

2. In a bowl, combine the bread with the meat, garlic, parsley, Romano cheese, eggs, and salt and pepper to taste. Form into 12 to 14 meatballs, about 2½ inches in diameter, and chill until ready to cook.

3. In a large saucepan or casserole set over moderate heat, heat the oil until hot. Add the meatballs and cook them until they're browned on all sides, 5 to 7 minutes. Add the marinara sauce and simmer, stirring occasionally, for 1 hour. Serve with your favorite pasta and freshly grated Parmesan.

BRACIOLE
Stuffed Meat Rolls

MAKES 4 TO 6 SERVINGS

1½ pounds flank steak, cut and pounded into thin slices about 4 inches wide by 6 inches long
Salt and freshly ground black pepper
½ cup freshly grated Parmesan cheese, plus extra for serving

4 cloves garlic, minced
½ cup minced fresh parsley leaves
3 tablespoons olive oil
4 cups Basic Marinara sauce (page 43)
2 pounds cooked pasta

1. Season the meat on both sides with salt and pepper to taste.

2. In a bowl, combine the ½ cup Parmesan, garlic, and parsley. Divide the mixture among the meat slices, spreading it into an even layer, and roll up each slice to enclose the filling. Secure each roll with string or toothpicks.

3. In a casserole set over moderately high heat, heat the oil until it is hot. Add the rolls and cook them, turning, until browned on all sides, about 5 minutes. Add the marinara sauce, bring it to a boil, and simmer the mixture, stirring occasionally, for 1 to 1½ hours, or until the meat is tender.

4. Transfer the meat to a platter and remove the strings or toothpicks. Return the meat to the sauce and simmer until heated through. Serve with your favorite pasta and freshly grated Parmesan.

LASAGNE

Leftover Sunday Gravy combined with ricotta and mozzarella cheeses in a lasagne is a great company dish, because you can make it the day before and simply reheat it for your guests. It tastes even better that way, when the flavors have had a chance to meld.

MAKES 8 SERVINGS

¾ pound fresh lasagna noodles (recipe follows), or 1 pound dried lasagna noodles

5 cups Sunday Gravy (page 98) or Basic Marinara Sauce (page 43)

2 pounds ricotta cheese

8 Meatballs (page 99), chopped

6 Italian sausages (sweet, hot, or a combination) cooked in Sunday Gravy, chopped

1 pound mozzarella cheese, grated

1. Preheat the oven to 350°F.

2. Cook the lasagna noodles according to package directions. If using fresh noodles, cook in a pot of boiling water for about 5 minutes. Drain and refresh under cold water. Arrange the noodles on layers of paper towels.

3. Spoon a thin layer of gravy in a large shallow baking dish, cover with a layer of noodles, and spread the noodles with a thin layer of ricotta. Sprinkle the ricotta with a layer of meatballs and sausages, and cover with a layer of sauce. Top with some of the mozzarella. Continue to layer the remaining ingredients in the same manner, ending with a layer of gravy and mozzarella.

4. Bake the lasagne in the oven for 45 minutes to 1 hour, or until it's bubbling.

LASAGNA NOODLES

MAKES ABOUT 1 POUND DOUGH, OR
ABOUT ENOUGH NOODLES FOR 1 LASAGNE

2 cups all-purpose flour
1 teaspoon salt, or to taste
2 large eggs, lightly beaten

1½ tablespoons extra-virgin olive oil
3 tablespoons water, plus additional if
    necessary

1. In a food processor, combine the flour and salt and process for 10 seconds. In a bowl, whisk together the eggs, olive oil, and water. With the food processor running, add the liquid ingredients and process until the mixture forms a dough, adding additional water if necessary. Process the dough for 20 seconds to knead. Let the dough stand, covered with an inverted bowl, at room temperature for 1 hour.

2. To roll out the pasta dough, set the pasta machine at its highest number (widest setting). Working with about 2 ounces of dough at a time (keep the remaining pieces under an inverted bowl), flatten into a rough rectangle. Sprinkle the rectangle with a little flour and feed through the rollers. Fold the rectangle in half and feed through the rollers 6 more times, folding in half each time and dusting with flour to prevent sticking. Turn the dial down one notch and feed the dough through without folding, turning the dial one notch lower each time, until the lowest notch is reached and the dough is a smooth, long sheet. Roll the remaining dough pieces in the same manner. Let the sheets dry for 30 minutes.

PITTI BOOP SANDWICH

Pitti Boop was the guy who cleaned up, along with my aunt Josie, in Pep's restaurant. I don't know his real name; he was a charity case, as we used to say, but not really. He did the work that he could do, and the community looked after him. His reward was a special sandwich made with the scraps of broken meat from the Sunday Gravy. And it was so delicious that we kids would ask for a Pitti Boop Sandwich, too, when we knew there was extra gravy around. Aunt Gracie thought that was funny.

MAKES 6 SERVINGS

Two 18-inch loaves Italian bread
½ cup Sunday Gravy (page 98)
1 cup pieces of various meats from
   Sunday Gravy (sausage, meatballs,
   braciole)

Salt and freshly ground black pepper

1. Split the Italian loaf in half lengthwise leaving one side hinged. Remove some of the inner crumb.

2. Spoon or pour the gravy over both sides of the open loaves and layer the meats on each loaf. Add salt and pepper to taste. Fold the 2 halves of the loaves together and cut into 6-inch slices.

ITALIAN-STYLE STUFFED ARTICHOKES

Everyone had a recipe for this. My brother Timmy's mother-in-law had the best one.

MAKES 6 SERVINGS

Juice of 1 lemon
1 cup water
6 whole artichokes
1 cup dry bread crumbs
½ cup freshly grated Romano cheese
12 cloves garlic, 6 finely minced, 6 smashed

3 tablespoons minced fresh parsley leaves
¼ cup extra-virgin olive oil
Salt and freshly ground black pepper
Six ½-by-¼-inch matchstick-size pieces of Romano cheese

1. In a bowl, combine the lemon juice and water and set aside.

2. Cut off the stem of each artichoke at the base and with scissors snip off the tips of the leaves. Dip the artichokes in the lemon water to prevent them from turning brown. With the palm of your hand, gently flatten each artichoke by spreading apart its leaves and opening it up like a flower. With a spoon, remove the chokes. Rinse the artichokes and invert them on paper towels to drain.

3. In a bowl, combine the bread crumbs, grated cheese, minced garlic, parsley, and 3 tablespoons of the oil. Season with salt and pepper to taste and mix the stuffing well.

continued

4. Working over the bowl with 1 artichoke at a time, pack the stuffing between the leaves and add a piece of the Romano to the center of each artichoke.

5. Transfer the artichokes to a casserole and sprinkle with salt and pepper to taste. To the pan, add 1½ inches of water, the remaining oil, and the smashed garlic. Braise the artichokes on top of the stove, covered, over moderately low heat, until they're tender, 40 to 50 minutes. Transfer the artichokes to a shallow baking dish.

6. Preheat the broiler. Broil the artichokes about 4 inches from the heat until they're golden brown, 1 to 2 minutes.

8

EASTER SUNDAY

Easter was the mother of all Sundays, and two or three times while I was growing up, my birthday fell on Easter, which made it even more festive. This was also the principal holiday for baking. Lent was the holiest time of the year, and Easter Sunday was the climax. The traditional Neapolitan Easter dinner features roast lamb and potatoes; so although we usually didn't have lamb in my home, I have included a traditional Neapolitan recipe for lamb here.

Young men on a feast day.

That's me, *second from the left,* in the Easter Pageant at Our Lady of Loreto.

Dedication of the statue of Franklin Delano Roosevelt.

Dignitaries on Pacific Street on a feast day.

'A PIZZA CHIEN'
Pizza Rustica

This spicy deep-dish meat pie is sometimes called "Easter Pie," because it is traditionally served at that time of year, or also "Pizza Rustica," because of its country origins. The name means "full pie" in the Neapolitan dialect, and we pronounced it *ah BEETS-a GAIN*.

MAKES 2 PIES, ABOUT 6 SERVINGS EACH

FOR THE CRUST

4 cups all-purpose flour
⅔ cup sugar
1½ teaspoons baking powder
1½ teaspoons salt
¾ cup (1½ sticks) cold unsalted
    butter, cut into bits
5 large eggs, beaten lightly

FOR THE FILLING

2 pounds ricotta cheese
6 large eggs
½ pound Italian dry sausage, thinly
    sliced and chopped fine
½ pound prosciutto, thinly sliced and
    julienned
¼ pound soppressata, diced fine
½ pound mozzarella cheese, diced
¼ pound provolone cheese, diced
½ cup freshly grated Parmesan cheese
Salt and freshly ground black pepper
1 large egg beaten with 1 teaspoon
    water to make an egg wash

1. To make the crust, into a bowl, sift the flour, sugar, baking powder, and salt. Add the butter and blend the mixture until it resembles coarse meal. Add the

eggs and stir the mixture until it forms a ball. On a lightly floured surface, gently knead the dough until it forms a soft but not sticky dough.

Or, to make the crust in a food processor, combine the flour, sugar, baking powder, and salt in the bowl of the processor and process for 30 seconds. Add the butter and process until the mixture resembles coarse meal. With the motor running, add the eggs in a stream, and process just until the mixture forms a ball.

2. Divide the dough in half, wrap each half in plastic, and chill for at least 30 minutes.

3. Preheat the oven to 350°F. Grease two 9-inch cake pans.

4. Working with 1 round of dough at a time, divide the dough round into 2 pieces, one two thirds larger than the other. On a lightly floured surface, roll the larger piece of dough into a ¼-inch-thick round and fit it into one of the cake pans, making sure the dough extends ½ inch above the rim of the pan. Prick the bottom with a fork. Roll out the smaller piece of dough ¼ inch thick and cut it into strips 1 inch wide. Chill. Roll out the remaining round in the same manner and chill while making the filling.

5. To make the filling, in a food processor combine the ricotta and eggs and process until smooth. Transfer to a large bowl and stir in the remaining ingredients, except for the egg wash.

6. Divide the filling between the dough-lined cake pans. Brush the edge (rim) of the dough with the egg wash and arrange the strips in a lattice pattern over each pizza, attaching the ends of each strip to the edge, over the filling. Fold down the extended rim of dough over the strips and brush the lattice with egg wash.

7. Bake the pies in the oven for 45 minutes to 1 hour, or until the filling is set and the crust is golden brown. Let them sit at room temperature for at least 30 minutes before serving.

ROAST LAMB WITH NEW POTATOES AND PEAS

The Neapolitans make this dish with either lamb or kid, but kid is a little harder for most Americans to come by. The roasted new potatoes, cooked along with the meat, are the perfect accompaniment.

MAKES 4 TO 6 SERVINGS

One 4- to 5-pound leg of lamb with
  bone
3 tablespoons olive oil
1 clove garlic, sliced
2 tablespoons dried rosemary leaves

Salt and freshly ground black pepper
2 to 2½ pounds small new potatoes
Two 15-ounce cans LeSueur peas,
  drained

1. Preheat the oven to 450°F.

2. Wash and dry the lamb. Place it, fat side up, in a large roasting pan, and rub the lean areas with 1 tablespoon of the oil. With a sharp knife, make small incisions all around the lamb and insert the garlic slices. Sprinkle with the rosemary and salt and pepper to taste.

3. Put the lamb in the oven and reduce the heat to 350°. Cook for 20 minutes per pound for rare, 25 minutes per pound for medium, and 30 minutes per pound for well done.

4. Wash and dry the potatoes and cut them, if necessary, into 1½- to 2-inch chunks. Coat the potatoes with the remaining 2 tablespoons of olive oil and add them to the roasting pan 45 minutes before the lamb is done. Add the peas for the last 5 minutes of roasting. The potatoes are done when a knife sinks into them easily.

HANDMADE ITALIAN RICOTTA CAVATELLI (ROLY POLIES)

As children, we rarely got to participate in the cooking, but our small fingers were just the right size for making cavatelli. The dough was rolled out and cut into small segments, which we then formed into the shell-like "roly-poly" pasta. By the time we were done, we had covered a damp tablecloth that had been laid across my parents' king-size bed. We ate the uncooked dough, and my mother warned us that it would grow in our stomachs. She wasn't worried about the raw egg back then. What did we know from Sal Minella—wasn't he some guy who delivered milk?

MAKES ABOUT 2 POUNDS PASTA

3 cups (1 pound) all-purpose flour
1 pound ricotta cheese

2 large eggs, lightly beaten

1. Put 2½ cups of the flour into a bowl, make a well in the flour, and add the cheese and eggs. Gradually work the mixture together, adding more flour if necessary, to make a soft but not sticky dough. On a lightly floured surface, knead the dough until it is smooth. Let the dough rest at room temperature, covered with an inverted bowl or wrapped in plastic, for 30 minutes.

2. Form the dough into a round and cut it into quarters. Working with one quarter at a time (cover the remaining dough with an inverted bowl to keep the dough from drying out), on a lightly floured surface, roll the dough into a rope ¼ inch in diameter. With a knife, cut the rope into ½-inch pieces. With your

index and third fingers held together, gently press down on each piece, begin-ning at the top and moving down toward the bottom, dragging your fingers to-ward you and causing the pasta to roll over on itself. Transfer the formed pasta to a lightly floured jelly-roll pan and let dry at room temperature for at least 30 minutes.

3. Bring a large saucepan of salted water to a boil, and add the pasta. Cook until the cavatelli are al dente, 6 to 8 minutes. They're done when they float to the top. Drain and toss the desired quantity with your favorite sauce. Freeze leftovers.

MANICOTTI

Baked Cheese-Filled Crepes in Tomato Sauce

In the Neapolitan idiom, the final syllable of many Italian words is cut off. Man-icotti, for example, is pronounced *mah-nee-GOAT*. But Neapolitans don't give short shrift to this delicious pasta. While we always cooked up dried pasta at the last minute, the manicotti crepes were prepared ahead. I'll never forget the sight and smell of the pancakes stacking up on the counter in my mother's kitchen be-fore they were filled and rolled. They were made for special occasions—on holi-days or when company was coming—and always in large quantities. Can there ever be too much of something this good?

MAKES 6 SERVINGS

FOR THE CREPES

1 cup all-purpose flour
1 cup water
3 large eggs
½ teaspoon salt
4 to 5 tablespoons olive oil

FOR THE FILLING

1 pound ricotta
2 large eggs, lightly beaten
½ pound mozzarella cheese, diced
½ cup freshly grated Parmesan
   cheese, plus extra for sprinkling
1 tablespoon minced fresh parsley
   leaves
Salt and freshly ground pepper
3 to 4 cups Basic Marinara Sauce (page
   43) or store-bought marinara sauce

1. To make the crepes, in a blender, combine the flour, water, eggs, and salt and blend, scraping down the sides of the bowl, until the batter is smooth. Transfer to a bowl.

continued

2. Heat a 6- to 7-inch skillet over moderately high heat until hot. Brush the skillet with about 1 teaspoon of olive oil to coat well and heat the oil until hot. Pour ¼ cup of the batter into the center of the skillet and lift and tilt the pan to coat the bottom with a thin layer. Cook until the batter is set and the underside is golden brown, about 1 minute. Turn the crepe over, cook until the underside is golden, about 1 minute more, and invert onto a plate. Make additional crepes with the remaining batter in the same manner. (Crepes may be made 1 day ahead. Cover and chill. Freeze for up to 1 month. Defrost in the refrigerator before using.)

3. Preheat the oven to 350°F. Lightly oil a large shallow baking dish.

4. To make the filling, in a bowl combine all of the ingredients, except for the sauce.

5. To assemble, lay each crepe on a work surface, attractive side down, spoon 3 tablespoons of the filling down the center, and fold in the edges to enclose the filling. Fill the remaining crepes in the same manner.

6. Spoon 1 to 1½ cups of marinara sauce into the baking dish in an even layer. Arrange the crepes, seam sides down, in the dish and spoon on enough of the remaining sauce to coat the crepes. (The dish may be assembled several hours or 1 day ahead. Cover and chill. Allow longer baking time if refrigerated.)

7. Bake for 15 minutes, or until the crepes are heated through and their edges are slightly crisp.

8. Sprinkle with additional Parmesan to taste and put the crepes under the broiler, about 3 to 4 inches from the heat, for 2 minutes, or until the top is golden.

DESSERTS

Most people in the neighborhood baked very little; few made a specialty of it. Among my aunts, Vee and Jenny were the bakers. You won't find recipes for lots of bread and cakes—for those, people went to the baker, Rose Sasso. Vee baked two kinds of things: simple cookies or holiday specialties. And when she did bake, she baked a lot: plenty of cookies and pies for the restaurant and family and friends.

An unwritten rule of the neighborhood was that the host never made dessert. If you were invited for dinner, you brought pastries from a bakery: cannoli, sfogliatelle, cookies, éclairs. There were several in our neighborhood: Ariola's, Caiazzo's, Sasso's. Rose Sasso's bakery was on Pacific Street in the basement of the building next to the social club. She did her baking in a brick oven, and the heavenly aroma of bread and pastries wafted to the street. Every Sunday, after church, I stopped by to pick up bread for my mother. And maybe I would pick up a cream- or jelly-filled donut for myself. Rose Sasso was a character. I remember her playing cards and joking and laughing with my mother and my aunts. Like them, she was a working woman. She had her own business and made a living—God bless her.

Even after we moved to Long Island, my father went back to the old neighborhood to buy bread on Sunday. We used some of it fresh then, and Mom froze the rest to use throughout the week. The Caiazzo Bakery is still there, but it now sells only wholesale.

GRAIN PIE
Lent Pie

Because it is traditionally served at Lent, this Italian custard pie is also called "Lent Pie." Since you have to give up something for Lent, this custard pie is supposed to ease your sacrifice.

MAKES 6 SERVINGS

4 cups milk

1 cup sugar

Pinch of salt

½ cup farina

6 large eggs, lightly beaten

1 teaspoon vanilla extract

1. Preheat the oven to 350°F. Butter an 8-inch square baking dish.

2. In a saucepan set over moderate heat, combine the milk, sugar, and salt. Bring just to a simmer and stir in the farina, a little at a time. Cook over low heat, stirring, until the farina has lightly thickened, about 5 minutes. Transfer to a bowl and let cool to warm.

3. Beat in the eggs and vanilla and transfer the mixture to the baking dish. Bake for 30 minutes, or until the top of the pie is golden.

ITALIAN CHEESECAKE

_Heavy and rich with the light tang of lemon zest, a little goes a long way.

MAKES 1 CAKE, ABOUT 10 TO 12 SERVINGS

FOR THE PASTRY

3 cups all-purpose flour
½ cup sugar
2 teaspoons baking powder
⅛ teaspoon salt
4 to 5 teaspoons grated lemon peel, or to taste
½ cup (1 stick) cold unsalted butter, cut into bits
4 large eggs, lightly beaten

FOR THE FILLING

2 pounds ricotta cheese, pushed through a sieve
1 cup sugar
6 large eggs, lightly beaten
1 tablespoon all-purpose flour
2 to 3 teaspoons vanilla extract, or to taste
¼ teaspoon ground cinnamon
1 cup heavy cream, lightly whipped
1 large egg beaten with 1 teaspoon water to make an egg wash

1. To make the pastry, into a bowl, sift the flour, sugar, baking powder, and salt. Stir in the lemon peel and butter and blend the mixture until it resembles coarse meal. Add the eggs and stir the mixture until it forms a ball. On a lightly floured surface, gently knead the mixture until it forms a soft but not sticky dough.

Or, to make the pastry in a food processor, combine the flour, sugar, baking powder, and salt in the bowl of a processor and process for 30 seconds. Add the lemon peel and butter and process until the mixture resembles coarse meal. With the motor running, add the eggs in a stream and process just until the mixture forms a ball.

continued

2. Wrap the dough in plastic and chill for at least 30 minutes.

3. Preheat the oven to 350°F.

4. Roll out two thirds of the dough on a lightly floured surface into a ⅛-inch-thick round, and fit it into a 10-inch springform pan. Roll out the remaining third of dough in the same manner and cut it into 1-inch-wide strips. Chill the dough while making the filling.

5. To make the filling, in a bowl, stir the ricotta, sugar, eggs, flour, vanilla, and cinnamon until well combined. Fold in the lightly whipped cream and transfer the mixture to the pan.

6. Brush the edge (rim) of the dough with the egg wash and attach the dough strips in a lattice pattern over the filling. Brush the lattice with the egg wash.

7. Bake the cake in the oven for 1 hour, or until the cheesecake is set and golden brown. Let cool for 30 minutes, and chill for at least 2 hours, or overnight, before serving.

ZEPPOLES WITH RICOTTA
Deep-Fried Ricotta Balls

Zeppole is the plural form of *zeppola,* but we gave them an English plural form by putting an *s* on the end. So we bastardized the Italian language. We did the same to English; we didn't discriminate. The zeppoles made by Aunt Jenny are a refined version of those served on the street during the feast of St. Joseph on March 19. A very similar cookie served at this time was called a *sfinge* (sphinx).

We had a lot of Josephs in our family—my grandfather Pep, my father, my older brother—and we used to go to St. Joseph's Church in Brooklyn for the feast-day celebration. Another popular coating, instead of confectioners' sugar, was cinnamon sugar. These zeppoles could kill you, they're so rich—so take it easy.

MAKES ABOUT 6 DOZEN

2 pounds ricotta
3 cups all-purpose flour
2 tablespoons baking powder
1 tablespoon granulated sugar
1 tablespoon vanilla extract

6 large eggs, lightly beaten
½ cup milk, or to taste
Vegetable oil for deep frying
Sifted confectioners' sugar for dusting

1. In a bowl, combine the ricotta, flour, baking powder, granulated sugar, vanilla, and eggs. Mix in enough milk to form a thick batter. Let rest for 30 minutes.

2. In a heavy saucepan or deep-fat fryer, heat 3 inches of oil to 350°F. With a spoon, drop tablespoons of the batter, a few at a time, into the oil and fry, turning frequently, until the zeppoles are golden brown, 3 to 4 minutes. With a slotted spoon, transfer the fried dough to a jelly-roll pan lined with paper towels to drain. Continue making zeppoles with the remaining batter in the same manner.

3. Before serving, dust with the confectioners' sugar.

9

CHRISTMAS EVE

Christmas Eve was more important to us than Christmas Day. Kids stayed up late, a lot of people went to midnight mass, we opened presents, and we ate. In Naples, Christmas Eve is celebrated with a huge seafood feast. In Brooklyn, there was a tradition of having seven fishes at this meal—one of which was usually *capitone*, a fat eel. But I have never really cared for fish, so the anchovies in my Pasta Puttanesca (see page 76) are my nod toward Neapolitan tradition. But I have included in this chapter recipes for Crab Sauce and Lobster Sauce and also for Fried Baccalà, the dried cod that is an Italian national symbol.

At the Rennys', Christmas 1967.

My brother Timmy carving the turkey on Christmas Day, 1967. With him is my cousin Richie Ciullo.

My brother Timmy on Christmas morning, 1949.

Shoveling snow.

CRAB SAUCE

I'll start with my sister-in-law's Crab Sauce, because even I could eat this when I was a kid. I'd have it with a little pasta just to feel part of the group on this special occasion. Here on the East Coast, we use the delicate blue crabs. If you live on the West Coast and use Dungeness crabs, you'll get a completely different and tangier flavor. Dungeness crabs also tend to be larger, so you might use only 8 to 10.

MAKES 4 TO 6 SERVINGS

¼ cup olive oil
12 cloves garlic, smashed
12 blue crabs, cleaned, claws
  separated from bodies
Two 28-ounce cans plum tomatoes,
  including the liquid, crushed with
  your hands

2 to 3 teaspoons sugar, or to taste
½ teaspoon dried red pepper flakes,
  or to taste
Salt

1. In a large saucepan or casserole set over moderate heat, warm the olive oil and cook the garlic, stirring, until it's golden, about 2 minutes. Add the crab claws and cook, stirring occasionally, for 5 minutes. Add the tomatoes with liquid, sugar, red pepper flakes, and salt to taste, and bring to a boil. Reduce the heat to low and simmer, covered, stirring occasionally, for 1 hour. Add the crab bodies and simmer, stirring occasionally, for 15 minutes more. Transfer the sauce to a bowl and let cool.

2. Chill, covered, overnight. Reheat and serve the sauce the next day over long thin pasta, such as linguine.

LOBSTER SAUCE

The Neapolitans refer to lobster as *lussuosa,* luxurious—and it usually crowns the Christmas Eve feast. This recipe is from Aunt Jenny, the famous baker.

MAKES 4 SERVINGS

¼ cup olive oil
12 cloves garlic, smashed
1½ pounds lobster, cut into pieces
1 small can tomato paste
Two 28-ounce cans plum tomatoes,
   including the liquid, crushed with
   your hands

¼ to ½ teaspoon dried red pepper
   flakes, or to taste
2 to 3 teaspoons sugar, or to taste
Salt
1 pound linguine

1. In a large, deep frying pan set over moderate heat, heat the oil until hot. Add the garlic and cook, stirring, until it's golden, about 2 minutes. Add the lobster and cook, stirring, until the lobster is red, about 5 minutes. Transfer the lobster to a plate. Add the tomato paste to the pan, and cook, stirring, for 2 minutes. Add the tomatoes and their liquid, the red pepper flakes, sugar, and salt to taste. Bring the liquid to a boil. Reduce the heat to low and simmer the sauce, stirring occasionally, for 30 minutes. Return the lobster to the pan and continue to simmer for 30 minutes more.

2. Meanwhile, cook the linguine according to the package directions, until al dente. Drain and transfer to a large bowl. Add the sauce and toss to combine.

UNCLE BACCALÀ

Even from the time I was just a little boy, I knew my uncle Meade Esposito was an important man; but it wasn't until I was much older that I realized how important he was. To me and to my cousins, he was mainly a funny guy who never seemed to take things too seriously. With twenty of us gathered around the table for a holiday dinner, he would start a food fight by throwing something at one of his nephews; then he'd sit back and enjoy the mayhem while the other adults tried

Timmy and his godfather, Meade Esposito, in front of Meade's 1950 Buick. They are standing in front of Pep's. In the background is the Palazzo di Napoli, where we lived, and Marino's grocery store.

Meade Esposito, *center*, with his friends and family in Pep's garden. On Meade's left is Ray Muscarella, Tony Bennett's first manager.

to calm things down. When I was seated near him, he would drop a piece of bread in my Sunday gravy, as if by accident, and then saying "Excuse me," he'd retrieve the bread after using it to mop up the sauce. He told the kids he didn't want to be called Uncle Meade. "Call me Uncle Baccalà," he said.

When I was older, I began to understand the sort of power he wielded as chairman of the Democratic party in Brooklyn. When it came to New York City politics, and even state politics, Meade was a kingmaker. He was an old-fashioned machine politician and he always delivered the vote.

I saw him frequently, not only at family gatherings but also at Pep's restaurant, which his mother ran. (Meade's father, Pep, had died in 1951.) Pep's was Meade's unofficial headquarters, where he'd meet with constituents, discuss problems, and solve them.

About a year after my family left the neighborhood and moved to Long Island, Meade persuaded his mother to close up shop. He bought a two-family house in Canarsie for his mother and two of his sisters, Josie and Gracie. Josie and her daughter Angela and Gracie's daughter Connie still live there. In his mother's basement, Meade built a restaurant-style kitchen, complete with a counter; and on the counter, he even put an old-fashioned cash register so she'd feel at home. As long as Felicia lived, Meade continued to hold court there, with his mother cooking for him and his cronies just as she had at Pep's.

A few years after Pep's closed, Meade's favorite niece, my mother, died, and that crushed him. The power broker was powerless to save her. But he could look after her family. I had just finished high school and was not doing anything to improve myself—in fact, just the opposite—and Meade asked me whether I wanted to go to college. I had actually made a feeble attempt to enroll in college; but the lines were long, so I decided to go to the track instead. I told him no, I didn't want to go to college. He knew the kind of guys I was hanging with at the time, and he asked me if I wanted to be a wiseguy. When I said yes, he cracked me across the face.

That's when he suggested I go into the restaurant business and continue the family tradition. I didn't know at the time that this was a defining moment in my life. He helped me get a job with Murray and Irving Riese, the brothers who started several chains, some of which (TGI Friday's, for example) are still operating. Meade suggested I move into Manhattan with my brother Joseph, who was trying to make up his mind whether he was going to be an artist or an actor. It turned out that I got quite an education, and I went from working for the Riese brothers to owning my own restaurant by the time I was twenty-one.

As many readers of this book already know, Meade was convicted of paying an illegal gratuity to his friend Representative Mario Biaggi. All Meade did was pay for a vacation for Mario at the Bonaventure Spa in Fort Lauderdale. The federal government spent years and millions of dollars trying to find some wrongdoing on his part, and that's all they came up with. Meade paid a hefty fine, and Biaggi went to jail. Quite honestly, I don't think Meade ever thought he had done anything wrong. He had grown so accustomed to power that he thought he was just conducting "business as usual." He made the kinds of deals that all politicians have to make and that the high-minded among us

Lefty Corozzo with a pair of striped bass for Christmas Eve.

find unforgivable. There is even a new generation of Italian-American politicians who look down on their predecessors, my uncle and others like him, and it seems hypocritical to me, because politicians like my uncle Meade helped make it possible for Italian Americans to enter the mainstream.

When Nelson Rockefeller was governor of New York—a Republican governor at that—he gave Meade a painting by Picasso, took it right off the wall and handed it to my uncle. Meade gave it back because Anna, his wife, didn't think it went with the decor, so Rocky sent him a black-and-white signed lithograph by Picasso in its place. Rockefeller even made a trip to Canarsie to visit Felicia and taste her famous cooking.

BACCALÀ

Salt Cod, Tomato, Onion, and Potato Casserole

There was a time when many types of fish were salted by the Neapolitans, but cod is the only one of these that remains today. Baccalà was considered "humble" food, but it was relished by all classes of Neapolitans. When I was a boy, I'd see the baccalà come into Pep's in wooden crates. It was the weirdest-looking thing—stiff as a board. It looked like petrified fish. The traditional method of de-salination is to put the fish in a big pot and put the pot under a tap and run a thin thread of cold water over the fish for 48 to 60 hours. Or you can use the method described below.

MAKES 6 SERVINGS

2 halves baccalà (salt cod), about 1½ pounds

Two 28-ounce cans plum tomatoes, drained and crushed with your hands, reserving 1 cup of the liquid

2 medium-large white onions, sliced

4 ounces Italian capers, drained

One 16-ounce can pitted black olives, drained

1 pound potatoes, sliced thin

½ teaspoon dried red pepper flakes, or to taste

Salt

1. Cut the salt cod into 4-inch-long pieces, place in a bowl, and cover by 2 inches with cold water. Soak for 2 days, changing the water once or twice. Drain.

2. Preheat the oven to 350°F.

3. In a 3-inch-deep casserole, layer the salt cod with the tomatoes, onions, capers, black olives, and potatoes, seasoning each layer with the red pepper flakes and salt to taste. Add the reserved cup of tomato liquid or water, cover loosely with foil, and bake for 30 minutes. Uncover and bake for 15 minutes more. Recover and bake for another 30 minutes, or until the potatoes are cooked through.

FRIED BACCALÀ

We served Christmas Eve dinner buffet-style with the Fried Baccalà on a platter. People just helped themselves to these tasty appetizers.

MAKES 12 SERVINGS

2 halves baccalà (salt cod), about 1½ pounds
Freshly ground black pepper
2 cups all-purpose flour

1 cup light or regular olive oil
5 lemons, cut into slices for serving
½ cup chopped fresh parsley

1. Cut the salt cod into 4-inch-long pieces, place in a bowl, and cover by 2 inches with cold water. Soak for 2 days, changing the water once or twice. Drain.

2. Lightly season each cutlet-size piece with pepper to taste and dredge in the flour.

continued

3. Heat ½ cup of the oil in a large frying pan. Over moderately high heat, fry the cutlets, adding more oil as needed, until they are golden brown on both sides, 2 to 3 minutes on the first side and 1 to 2 minutes on the second. Remove them to a platter covered with wax paper or paper towels and allow to drain.

4. Arrange the cutlets on a platter with the lemon slices on top, and sprinkle with parsley.

BACCALÀ SALAD

Here is yet a third way to serve baccalà.

MAKES 6 TO 8 SERVINGS

1½ pounds baccalà (salt cod)
8 cloves garlic, minced fine
½ pound jarred Tuscan peppers (peperoncini), drained, stemmed, and sliced
½ pound pitted black olives, drained and halved
½ pound green olives, drained and halved

Juice of 2 lemons
Grated rind of 1 lemon
⅔ to 1 cup extra-virgin olive oil
Salt to taste
½ teaspoon dried red pepper flakes, or to taste

1. Cut the salt cod into 4-inch-long pieces, place in a bowl, and cover by 2 inches with cold water. Soak for 2 days, changing the water once or twice. Drain.

2. In a deep skillet, cover the salt cod with water and bring to a boil. Reduce the heat to low and simmer until the fish just flakes, 5 to 7 minutes. Drain.

3. In a large bowl, combine the fish while it is still warm with the remaining ingredients, and toss to combine. Let cool, cover, and chill for at least 2 hours to develop the flavors.

STRUFOLLI

Honey-Coated Deep-Fried Dough Balls

Strufolli are among the most ancient desserts, probably brought to Naples by the Greek colonists who arrived more than 2,500 years ago. And these confections are an essential part of the Neapolitan Christmas festivities. Aunt Jenny's strufolli, like everyone else's, was baked in an aluminum pan, dripped with honey, sprinkled with colored confectioners' sugar, wrapped in plastic, and sent around to everyone—an Italian version of the fruitcake that gets passed around at Christmas, except that people actually loved strufolli.

MAKES 6 SERVINGS

continued

3½ cups all-purpose flour
1½ teaspoons baking powder
3 tablespoons sugar
1½ teaspoons vanilla extract
2 tablespoons dark rum
4 large eggs plus 2 large egg yolks
¼ cup vegetable oil, plus extra for
  deep frying

⅔ cup honey
½ cup sugar
1 teaspoon grated orange peel
1 cinnamon stick

1. In a bowl with an electric mixer, sift the flour, baking powder, and sugar. In another bowl, whisk together the vanilla, rum, eggs, egg yolks, and ¼ cup vegetable oil. With the mixer running, add the liquid ingredients to the dry and beat until the mixture forms a soft dough. Let rest, wrapped in plastic, for 30 minutes.

2. Divide the dough in half. Form each half into ropes about ½ inch in diameter, and cut each rope into ¾-inch pieces. Roll each piece into a ball.

3. In a heavy saucepan set over moderate heat, heat 3 inches of oil until a candy thermometer registers 375°F. Add the dough balls, in batches, and fry until they're golden, about 2 minutes. With a slotted spoon, transfer to a plate lined with paper towels and drain.

4. To make the coating, in a saucepan, combine the ingredients and cook the mixture, stirring occasionally, until the sugar is dissolved. Simmer for 3 minutes. Remove the cinnamon stick and stir in the dough balls. Transfer the strufolli to a serving dish and serve at room temperature.

GENNETS

Teardrop Cookies

Gennets were baked at Christmas and Easter, our most important holidays. The cookie is rather bland, but the anisette icing gives it a special kick.

1 cup (2 sticks) unsalted butter, softened
2 cups granulated sugar
6 large eggs
1 teaspoon vanilla extract
5 to 5½ cups all-purpose flour
5 teaspoons baking powder

FOR THE ICING

2 cups confectioners' sugar
¼ to ⅓ cup warm milk
Anisette to taste (optional)

1. In a bowl with an electric mixer, beat the butter with 1 cup of the granulated sugar until light and fluffy. Add the eggs, one at a time, and beat until combined well. Beat in the vanilla.

2. Into a separate bowl, sift the flour, the remaining cup of sugar, and the baking powder. Add 5 cups of the flour to the egg mixture and blend until a soft dough is formed, adding more flour if necessary. Halve the dough and wrap each half in plastic. Chill for 30 minutes.

3. Preheat the oven to 350°F. Grease 2 baking sheets.

continued

4. Pinch off 1-inch pieces from the dough, form into rounds, and place 2 inches apart on the baking sheets. Bake for 12 to 15 minutes, or until the cookies are pale golden. Let them cool on the sheets for 5 minutes, and transfer to racks to cool completely.

5. To make the icing, in a bowl, stir the confectioners' sugar with ¼ cup of the milk and enough anisette to form an icing thick enough to coat the back of a spoon. If not using anisette, thin with more milk. One by one, dip the tops of the cookies in the icing, letting the excess drip off, and return to the racks to set.

6. Store the gennets in airtight containers, separating the layers with rounds of wax paper. They will keep for about 2 weeks.

CENCI

Deep-Fried Bows

Among Aunt Jenny's cookies were the Cenci, which are easy to make but delicate, fancy, and fun for kids.

MAKES ABOUT 6 DOZEN

2 cups all-purpose flour
2 tablespoons granulated sugar
½ teaspoon baking powder
Pinch of salt
3 large eggs, beaten lightly, plus 3 large yolks

2 tablespoons vegetable oil, plus extra for deep frying
2 tablespoons dark rum
Sifted confectioners' sugar for dusting

1. Into a bowl, sift the flour, granulated sugar, baking powder, and salt. In another bowl, whisk together the eggs, yolks, 2 tablespoons oil, and rum. Add the liquid ingredients to the flour and blend until a soft dough is formed. Cover with plastic wrap or wax paper and chill for 30 minutes.

2. On a lightly floured surface, roll out the dough ¼ inch thick. Cut the dough lengthwise into strips 1 inch thick and crosswise into pieces 4 inches long. With a small knife make a slit in the center of each piece and then pull one end of dough through each slit to form bows.

3. In a heavy saucepan or deep-fat fryer, heat 3 inches of oil to 350°F. Add the bows, a few at a time, and cook them, turning, until they're golden on both sides. With a slotted spoon, transfer to a jelly-roll pan lined with paper towels to drain. Continue making bows with the remaining dough in the same manner.

4. Before serving, dust the cenci with confectioners' sugar.

RAISIN SPICE CAKE

Aunt Nancy's Raisin Spice Cake was a particular favorite of my uncle Meade. And once you taste it, you'll know why.

MAKES 1 CAKE, ABOUT 8 TO 10 SERVINGS

3 cups water
1 cup (2 sticks) unsalted butter or
    margarine
2 cups dark raisins
2 large eggs
3 cups flour
2 cups granulated sugar

2 teaspoons baking soda
2 teaspoons ground cinnamon
1 teaspoon ground cloves, or to taste
½ teaspoon salt
Sifted confectioners' sugar or
    chocolate frosting for garnish
    (optional)

1. Preheat the oven to 350°F. Butter and flour a 9-by-13-inch baking pan, shaking out any excess flour.

2. In a saucepan set over moderate heat, combine 2 cups of the water, the butter or margarine, and raisins and heat, stirring occasionally, just until the butter is melted, 3 to 4 minutes. Let cool.

3. In a large bowl, whisk together the eggs with the remaining cup of water. Stir in the cooled raisin mixture.

4. Into another bowl, sift the flour, granulated sugar, baking soda, cinnamon, cloves, and salt. Add the liquid ingredients and stir until well combined.

5. Pour the batter into the prepared pan and bake for 1 hour, or until a cake tester inserted in the center of the cake comes out clean. Let cool in the pan for 5 minutes and invert onto a rack to cool completely.

6. Garnish with confectioners' sugar or frosting, if desired.

INDEX

Aglio e olio, spaghettini, 75
anchovy fillets, in pasta puttanesca, 76–77
'a pizza chien', 110–111
artichokes, Italian-style stuffed, 105–106

Baccalà, 132–133
  fried, 133–134
  salad, 134–135
baked cheese-filled crepes in tomato sauce,
      115–116
basic marinara sauce, 43–44
beans:
  escarole and, 81
  pasta and, 87
  stringbean salad, 90–91
beef:
  in bolognese sauce, 48–49
  braciole, 100–101
  broiled steak, 21
  Joe Renny's stew, 68–69
  meatballs, 99–100
  red soup, 65
  steak pizzaiola, 22–23
bolognese sauce, 48–49
bows, deep-fried, 138–139
braciole, 100–101
  in Sunday gravy, 98–99
broccoli rabe with garlic and red pepper, 28
broiled steak, 21

Cacciatore, chicken, 67–68
cakes:
  Italian cheesecake, 119–120
  raisin spice, 140–141
cannellini beans:
  in escarole and beans, 81
  in pasta e fagioli, 87
carbonara sauce, 44–45
carrots:
  in bolognese sauce, 48–49
  in Joe Red's chicken meatball soup, 26–27
  in Joe Renny's beef stew, 68–69
  in lentil soup, 74
  in raisin spice cake, 140–141
  in red beef soup, 65
cauliflower and pasta shells, 50
cavatelli, ricotta, handmade Italian, 113–114
ceci, pasta e, 34
cenci, 138–139
cheese:
  -filled crepes, baked, in tomato sauce,
      115–116
  Swiss, and ham sandwich with marinated
      tomatoes, 89–90
  see also mozzarella; Parmesan; provolone;
      ricotta; Romano
chicken:
  broth, pasta e piselli with, 24–25
  cacciatore, 67–68

chicken (*continued*)
  coyote, 67–68
  cutlets and romaine salad, 35–36
  cutlet sandwich, 36–37
  francese, 37–38
  Joe Red's meatball soup, 26–27
  roast hunter's style, 67–68
chickpea and pasta soup, 34
children, pastina for, 52
clam sauce, white, 47–48
cod, salt:
  baccalà, 132–133
  baccalà salad, 134–135
  fried baccalà, 133–134
cookies:
  cenci, 138–139
  deep-fried bows, 138–139
  gennets, 137–138
  strufolli, 135–136
  teardrop, 137–138
  zeppoles with ricotta, 120–121
coyote chicken, 67–68
crab sauce, 126
crepes, baked cheese-filled, in tomato sauce, 115–116
croquettes, potato, 38–39

Deep-fried:
  bows, 138–139
  dough balls, honey-coated, 135–136
  ricotta balls, 120–121
desserts:
  cenci, 138–139
  deep-fried bows, 138–139
  deep-fried ricotta balls, 120–121
  gennets, 137–138
  grain pie, 118
  Italian cheesecake, 119–120
  Lent pie, 118
  raisin spice cake, 140–141
  strufolli, 135–136
  teardrop cookies, 137–138
  zeppoles with ricotta, 120–121
dough balls, honey-coated deep-fried, 135–136

Easter pie, 110–111
eggplant:
  parmigiana, 80
  pickled, 91–92
eggs:
  in 'a pizza chien', 110–111
  in carbonara sauce, 44–45
  in cenci, 138–139
  in gennets, 137–138
  in grain pie, 118
  in handmade Italian ricotta cavatelli, 113–114
  in Italian cheesecake, 119–120
  in macaroni pie, 66
  in manicotti, 115–116
  potatoes and, 78–79
  in strufolli, 135–136
  in zeppoles with ricotta, 120–121
escarole and beans, 81
Esposito, Meade, pasta puttanesca of, 77

Fagioli, pasta e, 87
fish:
  baccalà, 132–133
  baccalà salad, 134–135
  fried baccalà, 133–134
francese, chicken or veal, 37–38
fried:
  baccalà, 133–134
  deep, *see* deep-fried
  pepper "wet" sandwich, 88

Garlic:
  broccoli rabe with red pepper and, 28
  thin spaghetti with olive oil and, 75
gennets, 137–138
grain pie, 118
gravy, Sunday, 98–99

Ham and Swiss sandwich with marinated tomatoes, 89–90
handmade Italian ricotta cavatelli, 113–114
honey-coated deep-fried dough balls, 135–136
hunter's style roast chicken, 67–68

Italian cheesecake, 119–120
Italian ricotta cavatelli, handmade, 113–114
Italian-style stuffed artichokes, 105–106

Joe Red's chicken meatball soup, 26–27
Joe Renny's beef stew, 68–69

Lamb, roast, with new potatoes and peas,
   112
lasagna noodles, 103
lasagne, 102–103
lentil soup, 74
Lent pie, 118
lobster sauce, 127

Macaroni pie, 66
manicotti, 115–116
marinara sauce, basic, 43–44
meatball(s), 99–100
   chicken, Joe Red's soup, 26–27
   in lasagne, 102–3
   in Sunday gravy, 98–99
meats:
   bolognese sauce, 48–49
   braciole, 100–101
   broiled steak, 21
   Joe Renny's beef stew, 68–69
   meatballs, 99–100
   Pitti Boop sandwich, 104
   red beef soup, 65
   roast lamb with new potatoes and peas,
      112
   steak pizzaiola, 22–23
   stuffed rolls, 100–101
   Sunday gravy, 98–99
   veal cutlets and romaine salad, 35–36
   veal cutlet sandwich, 36–37
   veal francese, 37–38
meat sauce, 48–49
mozzarella:
   in 'a pizza chien', 110–111
   in lasagne, 102–103
   in manicotti, 115–116
   in potato croquettes, 38–39

New potatoes, roast lamb with peas and,
   112
noodles, lasagna, 103

Olive oil, thin spaghetti with garlic and, 75
olives:
   in baccalà, 132–33
   in pasta puttanesca, 76–77
onion, in baccalà, 132–133

Pancetta, in carbonara sauce, 44
Parmesan:
   in 'a pizza chien', 110–111
   in bolognese sauce, 48–49
   in braciole, 100–101
   in carbonara sauce, 44–45
   in cauliflower and pasta shells, 50
   in chicken cutlets and romaine salad, 35–36
   in chicken francese, 37–38
   in eggplant parmigiana, 80
   in macaroni pie, 66
   in manicotti, 115–116
   in pasta e ceci, 34
   in pasta e piselli, 24–25
   in pastina for children, 52
   in potato croquettes, 38–39
   in veal cutlets and romaine salad, 35–36
   in veal francese, 37–38
parmigiana, eggplant, 80
pasta:
   basic marinara sauce for, 43–44
   and beans, 87
   bolognese sauce for, 48–49
   carbonara sauce for, 44–45
   e ceci, 34
   and chickpea soup, 34
   crab sauce for, 126
   e fagioli, 87
   handmade Italian ricotta cavatelli, 113–114
   lasagna noodles, 103
   lasagne, 102–103
   lobster sauce for, 127
   macaroni pie, 66
   manicotti, 115–116

pasta (*continued*)
  meat sauce for, 48–49
  pastina for children, 52
  and peas, 24–25
  e piselli, 24–25
  prosciutto sauce for, 45–46
  puttanesca, 76–77
  raw sauce for, 51
  roly polies, 113–114
  shells, cauliflower and, 50
  spaghettini aglio e olio, 75
  Sunday gravy for, 98–99
  white clam sauce for, 47–48
pastina for children, 52
peas:
  in coyote chicken, 67–68
  in Joe Renny's beef stew, 68–69
  pasta and, 24–25
  roast lamb with new potatoes and, 112
pepper:
  fried, "wet" sandwich, 88
  red, broccoli rabe with garlic and, 28
pepperoni, in macaroni pie, 66
pickled eggplant, 91–92
pies:
  grain, 118
  Lent, 118
  macaroni, 66
piselli, pasta e, 24–25
Pitti Boop sandwich, 104
pizzaiola, steak, 22–23
pizza rustica, 110–111
potato(es):
  in baccalà, 132–133
  in coyote chicken, 67–68
  croquettes, 38–39
  and eggs, 78–79
  in Joe Renny's beef stew, 68–69
  new, roast lamb with peas and, 112
prosciutto:
  in 'a pizza chien', 110–111
  in escarole and beans, 81
  in pasta e fagioli, 87
prosciutto sauce, 45–46
provolone, in 'a pizza chien', 110–111
puttanesca, pasta, 76–77

Raisin spice cake, 140–141
raw sauce, 51
Red, Joe, chicken meatball soup of, 26–27
red beef soup, 65
red pepper, broccoli rabe with garlic and, 28
Renny, Gerard, pasta puttanesca of, 76–77
Renny, Joe, beef stew of, 68–69
ricotta:
  in 'a pizza chien', 110–111
  cavatelli, handmade Italian, 113–114
  deep-fried balls of, 120–121
  in Italian cheesecake, 119–120
  in lasagne, 102–103
  zeppoles with, 120–121
roast chicken hunter's style, 67–68
roast lamb with new potatoes and peas, 112
roly polies, 113–114
romaine salad, 36
  veal or chicken cutlets and, 35–36
Romano:
  in Italian-style stuffed artichokes, 105–106
  in Joe Red's chicken meatball soup, 26–27
  in meatballs, 99–100
  in pasta e piselli, 24–25
  in potatoes and eggs, 78–79

Salads:
  baccalà, 134–135
  romaine, 36
  romaine, veal or chicken cutlets and, 35–36
  stringbean, 90–91
salt cod:
  baccalà salad, 134–135
  fried baccalà, 133–134
  tomato, onion, and potato casserole
    (baccalà), 132–133
sandwiches:
  fried pepper "wet," 88
  ham and Swiss with marinated tomatoes,
    89–90
  Pitti Boop, 104
  veal or chicken cutlet, 36–37
sauces:
  basic marinara, 43–44
  bolognese, 48–49

sauces (*continued*):
    carbonara, 44–45
    crab, 126
    lobster, 127
    meat, 48–49
    prosciutto, 45–46
    raw, 51
    white clam, 47–48
sausage:
    in 'a pizza chien', 110–111
    in lasagne, 102–103
    in macaroni pie, 66
    in Sunday gravy, 98–99
shells, pasta, cauliflower and, 50
short ribs, in Sunday gravy, 98–99
soppressata, in 'a pizza chien', 110–111
soups:
    Joe Red's chicken meatball, 26–27
    Joe Renny's beef stew, 68–69
    lentil, 74
    pasta and chickpea, 34
    red beef, 65
spaghetti, whore's style, 76–77
spaghettini aglio e olio, 75
spare ribs, in Sunday gravy, 98–99
spice cake, raisin, 140–141
steak:
    braciole, 100–101
    broiled, 21
    pizzaiola, 22–23
stew, beef, Joe Renny's, 68–69
stringbean salad, 90–91
strufolli, 135–136
stuffed artichokes, Italian-style, 105–106
stuffed meat rolls, 100–101
Sunday gravy, 98–99
Swiss and ham sandwich with marinated tomatoes, 89–90

Teardrop cookies, 137–138
tomato(es):
    baccalà, 132–133
    in lentil soup, 74
    marinated, ham and Swiss sandwich with, 89–90
    in pasta e fagioli, 87
    in steak pizzaiola, 22–23
tomato sauce:
    baked cheese-filled crepes in, 115–116
    basic marinara, 43–44
    crab, 126
    Gerard Renny version of pasta puttanesca, 76–77
    lobster, 127
    pasta e piselli with, 25
    prosciutto, 45–46
    raw, 51
    Sunday gravy, 98–99

Uncle Meade's version of pasta puttanesca, 77

Veal:
    cutlets and romaine salad, 35–36
    cutlet sandwich, 36–37
    francese, 37–38

"Wet" sandwich, fried pepper, 88
white clam sauce, 47–48
whore's style spaghetti, 76–77
wine:
    red, in bolognese sauce, 48–49
    white, in white clam sauce, 47–48
Worcestershire sauce:
    in Joe Renny's beef stew, 68–69
    in steak pizzaiola, 22–23

Zeppoles with ricotta, 120–121